T0323993

Cambridge Elements ≡

Elements in Campaigns and Elections
edited by
R. Michael Alvarez
California Institute of Technology
Emily Beaulieu Bacchus
University of Kentucky
Charles Stewart III
Massachusetts Institute of Technology

A REPUBLIC IF YOU CAN AFFORD IT

How Much Does It Cost to Administer Elections?

Zachary Mohr
University of Kansas

Martha E. Kropf
UNC Charlotte

Mary Jo McGowan
UNC Charlotte

JoEllen V. Pope
Independent Researcher

CAMBRIDGE
UNIVERSITY PRESS

Shaftesbury Road, Cambridge CB2 8EA, United Kingdom

One Liberty Plaza, 20th Floor, New York, NY 10006, USA

477 Williamstown Road, Port Melbourne, VIC 3207, Australia

314–321, 3rd Floor, Plot 3, Splendor Forum, Jasola District Centre,
New Delhi – 110025, India

103 Penang Road, #05–06/07, Visioncrest Commercial, Singapore 238467

Cambridge University Press is part of Cambridge University Press & Assessment,
a department of the University of Cambridge.

We share the University's mission to contribute to society through the pursuit of
education, learning and research at the highest international levels of excellence.

www.cambridge.org
Information on this title: www.cambridge.org/9781009507387

DOI: 10.1017/9781009339452

First published 2024

A catalogue record for this publication is available from the British Library

ISBN 978-1-009-50738-7 Hardback
ISBN 978-1-009-33944-5 Paperback
ISSN 2633-0970 (online)
ISSN 2633-0962 (print)

A Republic If You Can Afford It

How Much Does It Cost to Administer Elections?

Elements in Campaigns and Elections

DOI: 10.1017/9781009339452
First published online: December 2024

Zachary Mohr
University of Kansas

Martha E. Kropf
UNC Charlotte

Mary Jo McGowan
UNC Charlotte

JoEllen V. Pope
Independent Researcher

Author for correspondence: Zachary Mohr, zmohr@ku.edu

Abstract: The cost of administering elections is an importantly understudied area in election science. This Element reports election costs in forty-eight out of fifty states. It discusses the challenges and opportunities of collecting local election costs. The Element then presents the wide variation in cost across the country with the lowest spending states spending a little over $2 per voter and the highest spending almost $20 per voter. The amounts being spent in the states are also examined over the election time period of 2008–16. Economic events like the Great Recession had predictable effects on lowering spending on elections but the patterns are not the same across the different regions of the country. The relationship between spending and election administration outcomes is also explored and finds that the voters' confidence and perceptions of fraud in elections is associated with the amount spent on election administration.

Keywords: election administration, election fraud, election confidence, election costs, elections

ISBNs: 9781009507387 (HB), 9781009339445 (PB), 9781009339452 (OC)
ISSNs: 2633-0970 (online), 2633-0962 (print)

Contents

Introduction   1

1 How Does One Measure Spending on Election
  Administration?   4

2 Election Administration Expenditures in the United States   23

3 What Affects How Much Is Spent on Election
  Administration?   38

4 Election Administration Expenditures and Election/Voter
  Outcomes   45

  Conclusion   64

  References   70

Introduction

Election administration is easy, right? It is just counting ballots. How hard could that be? That is what people that do not understand election administration think. How do we know this? We thought along these lines before we started studying election administration. We also know that people think election administration is easy because in the wake of the 2020 election, there were several attempts to recount ballots by hand by outside groups, and the complexity of the hand recount in places like Maricopa County were plagued with problems. To the hardened conspiracy theorist, this is evidence of a sinister plot to subvert democracy. To those of us who have studied elections for years or decades, a ballot recount failure is not at all unexpected. Election administration is a lot more complicated than it first appears.

People who work in elections, or who study them for a living, know several things about the complexity and difficulty of counting ballots that the nonexpert does not know. Nonexperts may only think about elections in the abstract and only periodically when their candidate loses. Unknown to nonexperts is the scope of elections. In a place like Maricopa County, there were millions of ballots cast and counted. Maybe a banker counts a million dollars by hand, but few members of the general public have ever counted anything into the millions. There are also different modes of voting. The reality of market-driven technology drives different modes of voting and changes in how we understand the advantages and disadvantages of different types of technology. Voting is complex. There are different rules for who can vote and how. A person with a sight disability has different needs relative to a person with mobility issues or someone with cognitive issues, but adults have the right to vote. Places with mail and early voting require signatures that must match. What do we do with people who come to the polling place who are not registered or do not have an identification? These are all challenges to the exacting practice of counting ballots. That final number that you see plastered on the television on election night is not the actual number but just an estimate that will change as the election administrators work to carefully sort out these issues, always under political scrutiny. The work of counting ballots and generally the work of election administration is not nearly as easy as it first appears.

People also think that measuring the cost of government services is easy. Surely, we know how much it costs to run elections in this country, right? How difficult is it to just run a report on the dollars that are spent to run the elections?

The truth is that we do not know how much it costs to conduct elections in this country. The scope and complexity of elections has limited analysis. In the United States, state and local governments administer elections, which means that there are over 8,000 local election jurisdictions conducting national elections. Mostly, election administration is conducted at the county level, but in some places the election jurisdictions could be cities, towns, villages, townships, and even two states are the local election jurisdiction. So, very large governments such as Los Angeles County California or Cook County, Illinois, with all of their capacity have much more advanced accounting than Pottawatomie County, Kansas.[1] Just like election administration, accounting for the costs of election administration requires judgments about what should count and what should not count. The different types of election administration lead to differences in the reported costs. A cost analyst needs to make decisions about the appropriate cost object and the length of the reporting period. So, there are different numbers one can examine, which lead to differences in the reported cost of election administration.

In the course of our work together, we have come to appreciate the similarities between election administration and government accounting. Counting dollars and counting votes are not that different. Accounting, reporting, and auditing all happen in the course of both elections and accounting, and they have to add up under intense scrutiny. Both election administration and government accounting are more complex and intense processes than the public ever imagines. There are also different numbers that matter in elections. Hillary Clinton won the popular vote and Donald Trump won the Electoral College. In government accounting, "expenditure" and "expense" sound similar but are importantly different as we discuss at length in Section 1.

The purpose of this Element is to start to answer the question of how much elections cost. How much does it cost to conduct election administration nationally? How much does it cost in different states and regions? Is the cost of election administration changing over time? What influences election administration costs and what impact do more financial resources have on outcomes? The manuscript seeks to give nonaccounting experts in the election administration community the language and the tools to talk about these different costs and to help nonaccounting experts to read the financial reports with a little bit more clarity about the different types of reports and the different types of costs that get reported.[2]

---

[1] Sorry Pot County, but you are always our example of a small county because both Martha and Zach went to undergrad close by and spent literally thousands of hours hiking your Flint Hills – we love you. Martha's parents kept cattle there. In fact, this Element is a kind of love note to the thousands of small places that work hard to uphold democracy and do not always get the love or the budget they deserve.

[2] Many people may want us to take these data and make inferences about how much local election officials should spend. Others want us to identify who is paying what when it comes to elections. Neither are the purpose of the present Element nor can these data tell us either. Rather, the data tell

To achieve these goals, the first section discusses the state of the literature and necessary accounting terminology. We argue in this section for our approach of examining the cost of election administration over the entire year and measuring cost as the actual expenditure rather than the budget. We then discuss the data that we collected and some of the many practical issues we addressed to make the data useful for comparison and analysis.

In Section 2, we descriptively discuss election administration expenditures in the United States. We explore the wide variation in expenditure from an average of just over two dollars in a couple of states to almost twenty dollars on average in other states. We then examine the cost of election administration over time, paying particular attention to the 2008–2016 period that is both "normal" from an election administration standpoint and a little bit abnormal from a government finance standpoint because of the impact of the Great Recession. We then compare the costs in different regions and how they changed significantly from the 2008 period to the 2016 period. We also discuss some of the within-state differences in cost at the local level. This descriptive analysis paves the way for the inferential analysis that follows in Sections 3 and 4.

In Section 3, we analyze some of the basic factors that influence the cost of election administration. For example, the literature has long known about economies of scale where the cost of election administration gets less expensive per person as the jurisdiction gets larger. However, many have also suspected that there was a point when the complexity and difficulty of administering elections in a very large jurisdiction may have additional costs. Because most of the previous analyses have focused on a single state, there is not enough variation at the large jurisdiction level in most states to test this hypothesis. However, our national sample allows us to test whether there are in fact nonlinearities to economies of scale.

In Section 4, we ask the "so-what?" question. What happens to election administration outcomes when some jurisdictions have more financial resources than others? Among other outcomes, we test the effect of election administration spending on voter confidence and perceptions of fraud. We analyze five things that may allow voters to connect financial resources to their overall perceptions about confidence and fraud – social scientists call these causal mechanisms. We also discuss the many things that election administrators do that the public either does not see or that scholars cannot capture with data such

---

us that there are vast differences in the amount local election officials expend to hold elections. Inevitably, this will cause inequities among different demographic groups, but to be honest, election scholars have long established that there are racial inequities and inequities based on wealth (e.g., Keyssar, 2009; Kousser, 1974). We do not need spending data to prove that point.

as administrative rule-following or voter education. These insights show us that a connection exists between expenditures and the perceptions of voters.

In conclusion, we highlight the limitations of our analysis and the opportunity for future research. Most importantly, we want to communicate that our estimate of election cost is a lower-bound estimate. We suspect that the full cost is much higher, but this herculean data collection effort provides a beginning point to discuss inputs and outcomes, particularly about what more spending might mean. We encourage those that would make use of our data to read and consider carefully the issues that we address in Section 1. We are making these data available at https://doi.org/10.7910/DVN/CSA1IL (to be published in open data repository when the Element is published) and encourage both researchers and practitioners to explore the data along with the analysis that we have done. In conclusion, we address some ways this research can inform election administration policy and practice. We hope that the election administrators will find some of these insights helpful in explaining to local legislators or the public why one might want to spend more resources on election administration.

1 How Does One Measure Spending on Election Administration?

It is not known how much we spend on election administration overall in the US each year. It is not known on what funds are spent. There has been little analysis of how and how well local governments provide election services. Each of us has some sense of what we get – a stable and successful democracy. But there are clearly problems that can be remedied. How much will improvements in this system cost?

– Caltech-MIT Voting Technology Project, Voting:
What Is? What Could Be? 2001, p. 48

In the aftermath of the 2000 election, the Caltech-MIT report *Voting: What Is? What Could Be?* estimated the cost of an election at about $1 billion over the entire United States, which they calculated to be about $10/voter (page 50). The report noted that localities spent more on solid waste management and parks than elections. They call their estimate a "ballpark" one, though the authors reported theirs was comparable to at least one other estimate (Hawkins, 2001). Yet, as was the case almost twenty years ago with much election-related data, there is no central location for election cost data, not to mention one standardized way to report such data. While academics and policymakers created more centralized data concerning voter turnout, provisional votes, and registered voters, we know of no scholars who have unearthed expenditure or cost data in a systematic way across most of the United States. Thus, there are basic questions that still have incomplete answers. How much do we spend on election administration and what influences that amount? While there are a few studies examining aspects of spending such as the cost of Colorado's election centers (Stein and Vonnahme, 2009), the cost savings from vote by mail (Lamb, 2021), and the factors related to spending in California (Hill, 2012) and North Carolina (Mohr et al., 2018), scholars are operating with limited cost data. What outcomes result from various expenditure levels in different jurisdictions is another question with incomplete answers. In theory and in limited analyses of a few states, we know that election administration spending can influence key election outcomes such as voter turnout (James and Jervier, 2017; Kropf and Pope, 2020) and election equity (Schur et al., 2017). What has been missing is a systematic analysis across multiple states, and in all the major regions of the United States. This Element seeks to start the conversation in this area of election administration.

In order to understand the resources required to run an election, and to work toward comparisons both over time and across states, in this Element, we report the election expenditure data we collected. We focus primarily on data gathered from annual financial reports (AFRs) and other sources of actual election expenditures such as state expenditure monitoring systems and the actual amounts spent as reported in local government budgets.[3] We provide some exciting results, but the overall purpose of this Element is quite technical. Because we hope readers will use these data, we share key decisions on our data collection, which are necessary to use the data.

This section first discusses previous research on election administration costs both in the United States and internationally. Second, we discuss the measurement issues inherent in unearthing local election administration cost data. Due to potential differences in accounting standards, there are a variety of problems when talking about the amount spent on election administration and the other services that local governments provide. Thus, this section reviews consequential issues related to the standards and bases of accounting, which are critical for understanding the possibilities and limitations of the different costs available in financial reports.

Furthermore, we also discuss the data collection process, the limits of the data, and the nuances that we have learned along the way. We have a case study at the end of the section that examines several features of election administration cost

[3] The data for this project were collected under two grants from the MIT Election Data and Science Lab and its funder, the Madison Initiative of the William and Flora Hewlett Foundation in 2017 and 2018. The fact that it has taken us this long to provide this analysis is a testament to the extreme complication of analyzing these data in a federalist system with over 8,000 local election jurisdictions with different election administration practices and methods, and in a federalist system with multiple forms of accounting. We have tried to harmonize the accounting and election data and make them understandable to the reader. However, some difficulties with these data remain intractable, especially in some states like Wisconsin and Michigan that are not included in the analysis. We hope that this Element will help spur others to examine the role of financial resources in conducting elections and to persuade policymakers of the need to further examine election administration funding in the United States.

data. The case study is an example of the complexity of collecting data on a diverse election administration system. The need for clarity and harmonization of the election and accounting research agenda that we discuss here could not be more important. We find that both election administration and accounting practices vary significantly at the local level from state to state and sometimes even within the state. This section is the foundation upon which to understand our data and our analysis. If you are planning on using our data, you will want to read this section and then examine the data at https://doi.org/10.7910/DVN/CSA1IL (to be published in open data repository when the Element is published), which has even more description on how we collected the AFRs and the data from all of the states.

Previous Research on Election Administration Cost

Research about election costs and spending has been tightly focused on a few jurisdictions (Montjoy, 2010) or certain functions such as the cost of election centers or types of convenience voting (Burden et al., 2012; Folz, 2014; Hamilton, 1988; Stein and Vonnahme, 2009). Nonprofit organizations such as the Brennan Center (2006) helped election policymakers (both state and local election officials) by estimating costs of particular inputs, such as voting equipment after the 2000 election. More recently, they estimated the additional costs of a pandemic on running elections during the 2020 election (Norden et al., 2020). Other organizations such as the Pew Center for the States conducted case studies of various states to understand costs.[4] Still others, such as California Forward and the ACE Project in Colorado endeavored to make cost data transparent to the public, but these important efforts all focused on a small number of states.[5]

Recently, political scientist Charles Stewart (2022) completed a comprehensive review of the question of the cost of elections. Stewart found that most of the recent estimates of the cost of election administration, including our previous analysis upon which this section is built (Mohr et al., 2018), converge on an approximate overall cost of approximately $2 billion to $5 billion spent on average every year. This is a fairly wide interval, but it is an improvement over the nearly complete lack of analysis of how much it costs to conduct election administration at the turn of the twenty-first century. However, these earlier estimates come from one or just a few states. In the subsequent sections, we discuss our more complete analysis of cost throughout the United States. We show there is great variation in expenditures per registered voter across and even within states. We find that election costs are

---

[4] See, for example, www.pewtrusts.org/en/research-and-analysis/articles/2013/03/19/the-cost-of-the-2012-general-election-in-wisconsin, last accessed July 12, 2018.

[5] See https://www.caceo58.org/election-costs, last accessed July 12, 2018. See also www.sos.state.co.us/pubs/elections/ACE/index.html, last accessed July 12, 2018.

changing, but those changes are very different depending on the region of the country. We confirm from previous findings that the "Great Recession" had an effect on election spending nationwide that was even more pronounced than thought earlier. We also show economies of scale pertain to the cost of election administration but that large counties exhibit diseconomies of scale. Finally, we learned that, even with high voter confidence between 2008 and 2016, more spending on election administration is associated with greater voter confidence.

It is not just in the United States where there is a growing interest in the cost of elections. James and Jervier (2017) show that many local election authorities in Great Britain are over budget. The increasing cost of elections paired with either very small increases in their budgets or reduced budgets increases pressure on officials. This results in cuts to election activities perceived as "noncore," including voter outreach and educational activities. They call for a "fundamental review of the financing of elections and electoral registration in the UK and in many other countries" (p. 7). Lopez-Pintor and Fischer (2005) provide in-depth research about the costs of elections in various democracies and provide key conceptualization of election costs. The research shows that there are differing costs depending on the status of the democracy (stable, transitioning, or post-conflict). Other scholars such as Aiyede and Aregbeyen (2012) examine single years in emerging democracies, such as Nigeria. Aiyede and Aregbeyen also examine nonmonetary costs such as loss of life due to elections. Of course, the status of democracy is not an issue about which those studying US election costs have historically worried, but these international examples underscore the high stakes of getting both election administration and the funding right.

The principal obstacle to US scholars studying election costs is not only the hyper-decentralization of elections but also the great variation in state laws and practices concerning budgeting, expense reports, and electoral institutions (that is, for example, that some states have early voting, some have by-mail voting, and various other nuances that affect the election activity and the funding of elections). We hope that providing these data across many states allows policymakers and scholars to see the financial impact of these different arrangements. We hope that others go beyond what this Element format allows and examine the differences in outcomes that arise because of differences in spending.

Valid Measurement of Cost

Defining Cost

In order to define what we mean by "cost," we discuss three elements: the jurisdiction (the who), the cost object or on what the jurisdictions are spending money (the what), and where we obtain the data with its inherent strengths and limitations.

The Who: Jurisdictions

The US Constitution delegates the authority and responsibility to conduct elections to the states, most of whom then delegate to lower units of government. Because these local governments have the authority to conduct elections, they are the units that primarily fund and report the spending on election administration. Thus, we examine the cost of elections in the lowest level of government that conducts elections in each state. Election expert Kimball Brace estimates that there are approximately 10,072 election jurisdictions in the United States.[6] For most states, the local government that conducts elections is the county, but cities, towns, villages, and townships also conduct elections. For the majority of states, the local election jurisdiction for federal elections is the county.[7] In the Northeast (Connecticut, Maine, Massachusetts, New Hampshire, Rhode Island, and Vermont), the local election jurisdiction is the township or city (1,620). More than 5,000 townships in the Midwest also operate elections (Brace, 2013). Two states in the Midwest have highly decentralized systems – Michigan and Wisconsin – and account for the majority of the townships that conduct election administration.[8] Michigan alone has more than 1,600 local election jurisdictions. Two states – Alaska and Delaware – conduct elections at the state level and they are included in this analysis as local jurisdictions because they are the lowest units of government that conduct elections.

The What: The Cost Object

While seemingly a simple question, "cost" is quite complicated (see Lopez-Pintor and Fischer, 2005) and there are a variety of items for which we want to know how much they cost. A cost object is "anything for which a measurement of costs is desired" (Horngren et al., 2012, p. 870). Instead of asking "how much do elections cost?," scholars often look at two cost objects of relevance: the cost

---

[6] However, almost 2,000 of these jurisdictions are jurisdictions that only conduct local elections. For example, College Park, Maryland conducts local elections separately from the federal elections, which are conducted by Prince George's County. We do not examine the jurisdictions that only conduct local elections. This is one way that we underestimate the total amount needed to conduct elections in the United States. Consolidating local elections with national elections may also be a way to save money (Durning, 2023).

[7] According to the Census Bureau, there are 3,144 counties in the United States but not all of them are the lowest-level jurisdiction involved in federal elections.

[8] Michigan had good election cost data at the township and county level. However, payments between counties and townships were often double-counted. The double-counting was not clear enough to develop what we thought was an estimate of election expenditures that were consistent with the other election jurisdictions in the dataset. Wisconsin had very small units of government from which collecting data was extremely difficult. Therefore, we exclude both states from our analysis.

of conducting an election and the cost of election administration. The *cost of conducting an election* is all of the costs needed in the window of time right around the election. The *cost of election administration* is the cost of an election plus the cost between elections that we measure as the total expenditures for all election activities throughout the year.

Some common examples of the cost of conducting an election include items that Caltech-MIT reported in determining the cost of running an election: "labor, maintenance, storage, acquisition of equipment, supplies (such as printing), information systems, and rental space" (page 49). Furthermore, election expert Tammy Patrick noted that there are a variety of election expenses that many do not consider. These include "processing of write-in candidates on ballots, a county deputy on call for potential election security calls, troubleshooting hotlines and other communications in case of troubles on Election Day" (Kropf, 2016, p. 43).

But what about the cost of keeping the election office open on a daily basis? It includes paying salary and benefits for the various employees on staff in the election office (FICA, workers' comp, retirement, medical insurance, etc.). Election workers must maintain voter registries, election equipment, conduct audits of the previous election, and organize for the next election. This often requires setting up contracts with vendors and polling locations or finding and training poll workers. The job between elections is perhaps less frantic but likely no less important to holding a high-quality election with minimal problems. We argue herein that the "cost of election administration" should include the cost of running elections, as well as the costs that elections offices have throughout the year as they prepare for elections and conduct their business between elections. Examining the cost of election administration throughout the entire year, as opposed to just the cost of conducting an election, is the inclusive cost that we focus on throughout the rest of the Element.

The Where: Sources and Standards for Local Election Administration Cost Data

We have argued elsewhere (Mohr et al., 2018; Mohr et al., 2020) that scholars should use the actual amounts spent on election administration as reported in AFRs[9] if they are interested in the cost of election administration. To briefly restate our arguments, the amounts that are reported in the AFRs are the actual amounts that jurisdictions spent on the election activity through the entire

---

[9] See Mohr et al. (2019) for the argument for why actual amounts spent are preferred to budgets and further explication of the different types of cost reporting. It is also worth noting that the actual amounts spent may also be reported in some budget reports, but these are usually the amounts actually spent for the previous year but are not audited.

fiscal year. The principal benefit of the total amount spent is that it is the actual amount spent and does not change. The budget can change and has been found to overstate the cost of election administration most of the time. However, that overestimate of the cost of election administration is not consistent over time as financial conditions can influence the amount of slack resources that can be provided in the budget (Mohr et al., 2020). Using AFRs to collect the actual amount spent also aligns with our "cost object" of the cost of election administration throughout the year in the reporting jurisdiction. Thus, we argue that the best source of administrative cost data is the data that come from AFRs.

To this point, the concept that we are describing sounds reasonably straightforward. However, the federal system of government does not make these financial comparisons easy. The accounting basis is the method by which government officials record and report financial activities. There are varying standards, that is, rules, of accounting used by US local governments. The two main standards for accounting are Generally Accepted Accounting Principles (GAAP), and Regulatory Cash Basis of Accounting (cash basis). Generally Accepted Accounting Principles is a standardized system that we will discuss throughout the rest of this section. Regulatory Cash Basis of Accounting is a catch-all group for accounting standards that are required by individual states and that are different from GAAP. Despite the lack of a unified standard across states, a sufficient number of states do require that their counties follow GAAP to allow comparison. And, as the discussion throughout the rest of this section indicates, cash basis accounting provides similar amounts that are comparable to GAAP amounts. However, the differences in the accounting standards can lead to some important differences in *some* of the amounts reported between the different standards.

Expenses versus Expenditures

They sound similar, but "Expenses" and "Expenditure" are technically different concepts. To find data on local election administration spending, we located "expenditures" in the Annual Comprehensive Financial Reports (ACFRs).[10] This represents one of the first decisions we made to locate cost data: the expense of election administration, which is a more "accurate" cost is simply not generally available. Thus, it is necessary for us to report that these data are a lower-bound estimate of what a local jurisdiction spends in a typical year. We make the argument that large capital expenses, such as voting equipment, did

---

[10] ACFRs are the audited financial reports of local governments that comply with GAAP. An ACFR is one type of AFR. Annual Comprehensive Financial Reports were formerly called Comprehensive Annual Financial Reports.

not happen often from 2008 to 2016, which makes the expenditures a lower-bound estimate.[11] We discuss the difference throughout the rest of this section to first justify our claim that our data are a lower-bound estimate and to make the case that by focusing on expenditures that our estimate of the cost of an election is similar across states that have different types of accounting.

Within GAAP there are two bases of accounting that local governments use – one to account for planned and implemented uses of money (govern*mental* funds) and one for accounting for the government as a whole (government-*wide* funds).[12] The first accounting method is the "modified accrual basis,"[13] which local officials use on governmental funds. Govern*mental* fund reporting is focused on the short term like a government budget and governmental statements are usually more detailed. The second method is "full accrual basis," which officials use for government-wide funds.[14] Government-wide funds are usually broader categories. For example, a "public safety" category might include police, fire, jails, and emergency management accounts. The public safety fund does not specify the dollar amount for each but an aggregate amount for all of the accounts. "Election administration" is almost always a category of "general government" or "government administration" in the government-wide statements. Therefore, it is not possible to pull out the full accrual expense of "elections" from the government-wide statements of the ACFRs.

Government GAAP accounting requires that government outlays are accounted for on a full accrual basis *only* in the government-wide funds.[15] However, government GAAP allows modified accrual basis in governmental funds.[16] Yet the full accrual basis as found in the government-wide funds would be the preferred method of accounting for the cost of election services. Why? Because the cost of

---

[11] This is why we restrict our analysis to after 2008 when jurisdictions spent most of the money from the Help America Vote Act (HAVA).

[12] For more information, please see Finkler et al. (2022) or www.gasb.org/page/PageContent?pageId=/standards-and-guidance/pronouncements/summary-statement-no-34.html.

[13] The term "modified accrual" is actually somewhat of a misnomer – modified accrual accounting has more in common with the cash basis of accounting than it does "full accrual" or "accrual" accounting.

[14] According to Granof and Khumawala (2013, p. 775) accrual basis is "[a] method of accounting that recognizes revenues when earned and expenses when incurred regardless of when cash is received or paid." For example, the "cost" of the voting machines is not an expense in the year it is purchased, but the expense is incurred over the useful life of the machine. If the machine has a useful life of eight years, then a straight-line method of depreciation expense would recognize one-eighth of the cost of the machine in each of the eight years of the machine's useful life. We will also call this the "full accrual" basis to distinguish it from the other basis of accounting.

[15] GAAP for US businesses requires the accrual basis of accounting that includes both cash outlays for noncapital purchases, depreciation costs of capital, and future liabilities that are incurred in providing activities, such as pension obligations, to develop the full *expense* of providing a specific service.

[16] The government-wide statements are inclusive of the governmental funds and also include the proprietary funds (i.e., business type funds), and component units.

voting equipment would be depreciated over the life of the equipment. Thus, the expenses would be matched or recognized when the service is provided and not when the bill finally comes due, such as the case of underfunded pensions. In contrast, the modified accrual basis recognizes the full cost of the equipment and outlays in the year in which the items were purchased and no cost thereafter for the purpose of matching the expenditures to the amounts stated in the budget. Because modified accrual accounts for the amounts spent out of the budget, modified accrual expenditures also have the same short-term focus as a government budget and cash basis accounting where the purpose of the accounting is to show budgetary compliance.

As noted, the government*al* statements in the ACFRs have more categories of detailed expenditures.[17] Therefore, we almost always observe the election administration cost in the modified accrual basis governmental statements.[18] Additionally, the supplementary information in the governmental statements also includes a comparison of "budget to actuals" for the governmental funds, which is where we often found election costs, and the "budget to actual" statement uses the modified accrual basis. It is important to note that election administration costs are almost always found in the governmental funds, modified accrual basis, and are thus short-term focused on *expenditures*. The costs for equipment are, therefore, lumpy and come in the single fiscal year in which jurisdictions purchase them. This is why we can observe election expenditures spiking after the passage of the Help America Vote Act in 2002 (HAVA).[19] If it were on a full accrual basis, these costs would have been spread over the estimated useful life of the equipment, but on the modified accrual basis the costs were recognized in the fiscal year in which the equipment was purchased. Also, other long-term liabilities such as pension and other post-employment benefits that are earned during the period may not be accounted for in the governmental funds.

The GAAP's modified accrual basis of accounting is similar to the Regulatory Cash Basis of Accounting (the non-GAAP accounting bases). They are similar in that they are primarily concerned with showing budgetary compliance, and are often different because of when they record financial events, or when they recognize that a cost has occurred. Costs recognized under the modified accrual

---

[17] Note that ACFRs have two types of statements. The government-wide statements that are on the full accrual basis and the governmental that are on the modified accrual basis. The full accrual cost estimates are called expenses and modified accrual are called expenditures. Regulatory basis and cash accounting cost estimates are also expenditures.

[18] We have found one case of reporting election expenses in the government-**wide** statements in all of the thousands of reports that we have located. Only Cook County, Illinois, provides both election administration expenditure and expense and, as can be seen in their financial statements, the expenditures are lower than the expenses.

[19] In North Carolina, this was 2006 and 2007.

basis are "expenditures." Cash accounting also records "expenditures" and not "expenses." Over multiple years, the "expenditures" in the modified accrual basis would be substantially similar to the "expenditures" in a cash basis.

The picture that emerges when we look at the post-HAVA modified accrual expenditures is that they are a consistently lower-bound estimates of the resources needed to finance election administration. The key benefit is that they are the actual amounts that were spent and correspond with the resource control purposes of the annual budget and comparable to the regulatory cash basis.

We hope the reader can see that full accrual would be strongly preferred as a measure of the full resources consumed in the production of election administration because it would spread out the capital costs of election equipment over the useful life of the equipment and match the other long-term costs incurred in delivering the service. However, the amount spent on election administration in a jurisdiction is almost never recognized in the government-wide (full accrual) statements. It is also important to note that governments are often not required to split out the costs for election administration, even in governmental funds. While some states have financial reports for jurisdictions to fill out that require local jurisdictions report their election administration expenditures,[20] the majority of states leave the governmental funds detail to the discretion of the local jurisdiction. Therefore, many jurisdictions simply roll the election administration expenditures into a broader category of general government and do not report election administration separately.[21]

In summary, we have discussed the sources of *local elections* cost data, which varies significantly throughout the United States. We then discussed our cost object as the entire amount that was spent on election administration throughout the entire year or *the cost of elections administration*. We then discussed why the cost that we use is the *expenditures* on election administration and the limitation of expenditures being that they are a lower-bound estimate of the cost of election administration in local governments in the United States over this time.

Data, Methods, and Analysis

Data

As already noted, the data for this study come from the AFRs of the election jurisdictions in forty-eight out of fifty states.[22] The sources of data and

---

[20] That is, North Carolina, New York, California, Indiana.

[21] Because there is no way to collect the election costs from these aggregate totals, these amounts are coded as missing in the dataset.

[22] AFRs are inclusive of both GAAP-based ACFRs and the regulatory financial reporting of non-GAAP states. As stated in footnote 3, Michigan and Wisconsin are not included in this analysis because of comparability and availability issues.

a discussion of how the data were collected for each individual state at the time of collection can be found in the data codebook.

In a few states (i.e., North Carolina, California, New York, Washington state, Indiana), the state collects the expenditure for election administration in a larger database of county expenditures. Where the state already has a database of county expenditures and it includes election costs, we use the expenditure amount in the state's database. In our data collection process, the most often-found source of AFRs was a state or university website that put individual county AFRs, usually in pdf form, on a website. We then downloaded and searched each individual AFR for the term "election." If the term was not searchable, we visually reviewed the government-wide statements, the governmental statements, and the governmental detailed statements found in the supplemental information of the AFR, particularly the budget to actual statement. In a few cases, we went to individual jurisdiction websites to find AFR information (see also Mohr et al., 2018). In subsequent stages of data collection, we followed similar procedures as those already noted but, in some cases, we had to use the actual amounts noted in the budgets.[23]

In the process of cleaning and checking the data, we found that some costs seemed too low compared with other jurisdictions in their state or jurisdictions of similar size. We realized when checking these costs that the costs had been recorded from special revenue funds. These are funds that are set aside from a special source of revenue such as a dedicated property or sales tax to fund a specific activity. The purpose of the special revenue varies. In a place like Harris County, Texas, we found that the special revenue was a very small portion of the total amount expended on election administration. Therefore, all costs that we found that had come from special revenue funds and were significantly lower were coded as missing. Where we could find actual amounts spent, as was the case in some of the Harris County budgets, we used the reported actual amounts in the budget.[24]

To standardize the data across jurisdictions as much as possible, we also needed to locate election data. Simply put, large urban jurisdictions spend more than small rural jurisdictions, so we needed some way to compare them on spending. Thanks to the Election Assistance Commission and the Election Administration and Voting Survey, finding information about the number of registered voters in each county or township was not difficult. From the EAVS

---

[23] As already noted, because the cost comes from the governmental funds and are total expenditures, the accounting should be equivalent between the actual amounts spent as reported in the budget and the amount reported in an AFR statement such as the budget to actual statements.

[24] This resulted in spending per person that was in line with other jurisdictions' spending in the state.

data, we are also able to obtain the number of ballots cast in each jurisdiction.[25] Where these data are not available, we went directly to state and local Secretary of State or Election Board websites. A notable example is North Dakota, where there is no voter registration, and therefore no "number of registered voters" available. However, visiting the North Dakota SOS website, the state has "number of eligible voters" which we felt was close enough, given this is the number that local election officials must plan for when administering an election. Therefore, we can compare costs across jurisdictions, according to the expenditure per registered voter.

Statistical Methods

The methods used to analyze the data are basic descriptive statistics and hierarchical (multilevel or mixed effects) models (Gelman and Hill, 2010). Because the units we analyze are election jurisdictions nested in states, the data have a hierarchical data structure. We use hierarchical models to test the economies and diseconomies of scale at the local level between election spending and the number of registered voters of the election jurisdiction. Because the unit of analysis in Section 4 is individuals and their perceptions of elections, these individual responses are nested in election jurisdictions that are nested in states. This necessitates that we use a multilevel hierarchical model with random effects for states and election jurisdictions. All models include year fixed effects.

Nonresponse Analysis

A big question for our dataset is how much data for each state were we able to collect? The worry is that the counties for which we could collect data are not representative of all counties. We do not want to only analyze data from large and well-resourced jurisdictions as that would not allow us to make conclusions about jurisdictions that may have resource constraints. We tried to collect data from every jurisdiction, but there were many reasons why we could not for some jurisdictions. Some do not make their financial reports available or are not required to by their states. This is particularly true of small jurisdictions. Some places had financial reports available, but election expenditures were not listed in the financial report because they were included with "general government" or the category that was broadly labeled "administration." Finally, a small number of jurisdictions had only spending from special revenue

---

[25] www.eac.gov/research-and-data/datasets-codebooks-and-surveys. Last accessed September 18, 2023. We obtain registered voters from "all registered voters" rather than either "active" or "inactive" with the intent of standardizing across jurisdictions. Not all jurisdictions separate active and inactive registered voters in their reports for EAVS.

funds provided in their financial reports and so we omitted these. All these reasons may make some types of governments, particularly larger ones, more likely to be included in the dataset. The size of the jurisdiction is particularly important in all cases. Larger jurisdictions tend to have more capacity and are more likely to provide more financial information relative to very small jurisdictions (Kropf et al., 2020). However, we also noted a pattern where some of the very largest jurisdictions also were not providing the election expenditure data (i.e., Tennessee).

To address our concerns about nonrandom missing data that may bias the findings in Section 4, we conducted a nonresponse analysis of substantially collected states.[26] In other words, we compared the jurisdictions for which we had data to those we did not. The analysis focuses on the period from 2008 to 2016 (which gives us three presidential election years to consider). We needed to collect the data in the majority of the jurisdictions for at least five out of the nine years. We first focused on states that had at least 55 percent of the jurisdictions collected. We conducted regression analysis for each of these states, analyzing whether we had data for the election jurisdiction or not.[27] We analyzed whether the data availability relates to the jurisdiction size in terms of the number of registered voters. In concept, we do not want to see a significant relationship because the size of the jurisdiction may also be a proxy for the capacity of the organization, as already mentioned. We use all of the data for all forty-eight states for Section 2 and Section 3. For Section 4 we include in our analysis only the states with high levels of election costs collected, which we finalized at 75 percent collection,[28] and that are not significantly related to the size of the jurisdiction. The nine states used in Section 4 that matched these criteria include Alaska, California, Iowa, Maryland, Nebraska, North Dakota, New York, South Dakota, and Washington (See Table 1). Readers and analysts who want to use our data should be very cautious when using election cost data outside of these nine states.

Four other states passed these criteria for a subset of years. For example, Florida and Indiana counties started reporting in centralized collection

---

[26] We use the full sample in Section 2 because it is basic descriptive statistics. Section 3 is an inferential analysis where we need to be concerned about missing data bias, but we took the additional step to rerun the analyses on the sample that passed the nonresponse analysis and the results are not substantially different.

[27] We use binary logistic regression appropriate for a dependent variable with two categories.

[28] Most of the jurisdictions between 55 percent and 75 percent collected failed the analysis but only a few above that threshold failed the analysis: NC and TN. North Carolina also passed when restricted to 2008–2014 and is included in a secondary analysis that we conducted for robustness purposes to see if our results held with these additional observations.

Table 1 Nonresponse analysis table of inclusion and percent collected

State	Included in primary analysis	% collected 2008–2016	Secondary analysis	% collected subset years	Subset years
AK	YES	100.00%	*		
AL		1.99%			
AR		4.16%			
AZ		68.89%			
CA	YES	89.83%	*		
CO		21.01%			
CT		53.20%			
DE		70.00%	YES	100.00%	2008–2014
FL		57.33%	YES	76.63%	2011–2016
GA		66.94%			
HI		28.89%			
IA	YES	89.90%	*		
ID		23.18%			
IL		21.85%			
IN		70.17%	YES	90.22%	2011–2016
KS		71.64%			
KY		2.17%			
LA		68.06%			
MA		1.85%			
MD	YES	92.08%	*		
ME		2.72%			
MN		41.38%			
MO		38.81%			
MS		12.39%			
MT		3.39%			
NC		86.90%	YES	97.29%	2008–2014
ND	YES	100.00%	*		
NE	YES	78.17%	*		
NH		7.93%			
NJ		64.88%			
NM		4.24%			
NV		39.41%			
NY	YES	87.62%	*		
OH		39.14%			
OK		50.07%			

Table 1 (cont.)

State	Included in primary analysis	% collected 2008–2016	Secondary analysis	% collected subset years	Subset years
OR		33.06%			
PA		10.60%			
RI		53.20%			
SC		40.49%			
SD	YES	98.03%	*		
TN		89.05%			
TX		29.45%			
UT		57.76%			
VA		26.69%			
VT		9.67%			
WA	YES	88.03%	*		
WV		7.64%			
WY		40.00%			

*Included in both primary and secondary analysis.

systems after 2010 and therefore entered our dataset after that time. Delaware showed its election cost in its budget prior to 2015, but at that time began aggregating the cost with general government, which meant that we no longer could find the costs in its financial reports. Finally, North Carolina failed the nonresponse analysis for the years 2008–2016, but when we ran it on the years prior to 2014, years on which we have previously written (i.e., Mohr et al., 2018), it passed the nonresponse test. Because we must make significant caveats about these secondary states, we first report all tests in Section 4 on the nine states from the primary analysis that are substantially collected for all years and that pass the nonresponse test. However, we also run secondary tests, including the secondary states, to make sure the results are similar. Thus, the total sample of states in the secondary analysis is thirteen states, which includes the nine from the primary analysis and Delaware, Florida, Indiana, and North Carolina. (In time and with additional data collection, some of these secondary states may also be useful for analysis like the nine states in the primary analysis. The election cost analyst is warned to be sensitive to issues of nonresponse and missingness in these data.)

Election Year Adjusted Fiscal Years: Introducing the E-FY

The effect of the timing of financial reporting on election administration cost is a subtle but important complication that we also address. This is necessary especially when we want to examine the effect of resources on election administration outcomes. In this section, we describe the problem and then we discuss how we adjust for it in the analysis in Section 4.[29]

Put simply, the end of the fiscal year is especially complicating for analysis with elections when the majority of the cost of election administration happens in the months leading up to the general election in November. Many states require that their counties'[30] fiscal year end on June 30 (i.e., North Carolina), coinciding with their states' fiscal year end. Many other states require a fiscal year ending at the end of the calendar year – December 31 (i.e., Kansas). Some states do not have a requirement for end of the year fiscal reporting for counties and the counties can choose any month they want to end their fiscal year (i.e., Georgia). Due to this, at least one election jurisdiction in our dataset has a fiscal year ending every month of the year with the exception of February, which is probably because it is a short month.

Even though almost every month is a fiscal year end for some election jurisdiction, the problem can be summarized succinctly by considering the two most common fiscal year end months: June (53 percent of observations) and December (30 percent of observations). For December, the fiscal year aligns quite well with the election year. The majority of the cost comes in the months leading up to the election in November, and the December fiscal year end also captures the cost of the primaries that are several months earlier but can still be a substantial – and costly – effort. Therefore, the December (and November) fiscal year end captures the cost of the general election and the primary in that election year. The election jurisdictions that have fiscal year ends in June, on the other hand, do not match well with the election year. For example, if we want to obtain the cost of election administration for a jurisdiction with a June fiscal year end that captures the 2016 election that takes place in November 2016, we have to look at their financial statements from fiscal year 2017 because fiscal year 2017 runs from July 1, 2016, to June 30, 2017. This

---

[29] In Sections 2 and 3, we use the jurisdiction fiscal year to show year-to-year variation, even though the problems that we discuss in this section also complicates comparison across jurisdictions with different fiscal years. The reason that we do this is that our solution to matching resources requires two years of data for the election administration cost to make the resources of jurisdictions that report at different times comparable. We have analyzed the election costs in Sections 2 and 3 with both the fiscal year and the election year adjusted fiscal year, and the trends that we discuss are similar.

[30] This applies to election jurisdictions generally, but here we will discuss the simplifying case of counties to make the discussion easier to follow.

applies to all election jurisdictions that have fiscal years that end before November. It is especially confounding for states like North Carolina that have fiscal year ends that fall between the general election and the primary. Most of the cost of the election happens in November but there is some nontrivial amount of cost for the primary that we would ideally like to capture because this cost is captured in the jurisdictions with fiscal year ends in December.

To make the costs more comparable, we aggregate the expenditure from the fiscal year that corresponds with the election year with the prior fiscal year.[31] The specific decision criteria that we use to make our election year adjusted fiscal years (E-FY) variable is as follows. For any jurisdiction that has a fiscal year end less than November (January–October), we use the fiscal year after the election (i.e., fiscal year 2017 because it captures the November 2016 election) and add that with the fiscal year of the election to capture the cost of the primary (i.e., fiscal year 2016). However, we need to make the pre-November jurisdictions similar to the jurisdictions with fiscal years ending in November and December. To accomplish this, we add the amount spent in the year of the election (i.e., fiscal 2016) to the amount spent in the year preceding it (i.e., fiscal year 2015).[32] The result of adding the two fiscal years in this way is that we capture the fiscal year associated with the general election and the fiscal year of the nongeneral election year. In this way, we capture two years of fiscal data for the E-FY, but it captures a comparable expenditure amount for purposes of matching with general election year outcomes in jurisdictions with different fiscal years.

In this section, we reviewed our methodology for creating the E-FY, our data collection, and our rationale for cost of an election and cost of election administration. Next we provide an example of the detailed and exacting data collection process to shed light on how this process works as well as give an example of our decision-making process.

---

[31] Here, we follow an approach similar to that employed in our earlier paper (Kropf et al., 2020). However, we use two years of election expenditure to be able to examine both presidential and congressional elections instead of aggregating four years of data to focus on just presidential elections.

[32] In practical terms, this approach is defensible because the start of the E-FY will begin in the same calendar year and includes the cost from one general election year and one nongeneral election year. For example, the beginning of the 2016 E-FY for the jurisdictions with June fiscal year ends starts in July 2015, and the 2016 E-FY for jurisdictions with December fiscal year ends starts in January 2015. The approach also captures the cost of a general election year with the cost of a nongeneral election year. Given that we believe that general elections have significantly more costs than the nongeneral election years, the E-FY for these two jurisdictions should be very similar. The primary concern is inflation, but we have adjusted the expenditure amount for inflation.

Case Study: The Clerk and Election Administration or Just the Cost of Election Administration

In the process of validating the data, we came upon a large outlier in Wyoming: The cost of the County Clerk in Campbell County was labeled Clerk-Elections. In some communities, this may be the clerk of elections, but in this case, it was the county clerk *and* elections. Normally, we would not have been able to use this "cost" as it is clearly more than the cost of election administration. County clerks do a variety of activities such as recording deeds, issuing marriage licenses, even issuing animal permits in some places, as well as being responsible for election administration in many places. Thus, when election costs are separate, we include them; when they are combined with the entire County Clerk office, we exclude them.

Campbell County, Wyoming, is an exception in that we can clearly tell from the financial documents that the election administrator is *part* of the Clerk's Office but the cost of the election administration is also reported separately. From this we can see that election administration in Campbell County is about 9 percent of the Clerk's budget (Table 2). However, during general election years that amount (average 11.5 percent) is significantly more than the non-general election years (average 5.9 percent). The reason for this is the significant increase in expenditures that come with a general election. The point is that we

Table 2 Cost of elections in Campbell County, Wyoming

County	Fiscal year	Election year*	Clerk-elections	Elections	Election % of clerk cost
Campbell	2007	2006	$1,775,072	$212,643	11.98
Campbell	2008	2007	$1,940,366	$144,836	7.46
Campbell	2009	2008	$2,038,385	$236,454	11.60
Campbell	2010	2009	$2,038,385	$102,121	5.01
Campbell	2011	2010	$2,238,966	$251,084	11.21
Campbell	2012	2011	$2,255,062	$143,275	6.35
Campbell	2013	2012	$2,457,449	$301,747	12.28
Campbell	2014	2013	$2,513,865	$128,667	5.12
Campbell	2015	2014	$2,690,905	$329,251	12.24
Campbell	2016	2015	$2,508,185	$134,635	5.37
Campbell	2017	2016	$2,542,464	$249,798	9.83
Average			$2,272,646	$203,137	8.95

*FY end is June.

cannot use the County Clerk's expenditure. "Clerk" costs are fairly stable; but "election administration" costs are much more volatile, at least on a year-to-year basis. This also shows why we are missing costs in some small, rural jurisdictions that simply combine the cost of election administration with the total cost of running the county clerk's office.

Conclusion

We made many decisions on how to conceptualize the cost of elections and how to collect the data in a way that is comparable across jurisdictions and states. We argue we should measure "the total amount spent on election administration" and use the expenditures reported in the jurisdictions' financial statements to do so. From a practical standpoint, collecting the "total election expenditure" is justified because it is the amount that is provided in the vast majority of financial statements we located and it facilitates comparison across the state. The downside to expenditures is that they tend to underestimate the cost of election administration because expenditures account for the entire cost of capital equipment in the year in which it was purchased and may leave out some important costs like health care and pension costs. This is why we restrict most of our analysis to the period after 2007 when most of the HAVA spending had already occurred.[33]

Despite many challenges, we collected data for a significant number of election jurisdictions over multiple years. We collected election administration expenditures from local election jurisdictions from forty-eight out of fifty states. These data form the core of the data for the analyses in Sections 2 and 3. We also have data from a significant number of jurisdictions in nine states (and four additional states that are not over the entire eight-year span) that are appropriate for analysis with administrative election outcomes in Section 4.

In conclusion, this section describes the major decisions that we made regarding the data to guide others in analyzing the data. At times we felt that putting this all together was a puzzle that was too difficult and that had too many missing pieces. The puzzle seemed gargantuan and unwieldy. After years of struggling with these data, we are convinced that the pieces that we have been able to put together are important enough to describe here. We hope that this is only the beginning of the analysis and that others can take our descriptions and help us begin to collect and analyze the missing pieces.

---

[33] The exception to this is the analysis of the impact of the Great Recession, which like our earlier paper we use the years 2005–2016, but we also rerun the analysis on only the post-2007 period to be like the rest of the Element.

2 Election Administration Expenditures in the United States

Election administration observers have noted for a long time that there are differences across states, across election jurisdictions within states, and even across precincts. In his report *The Cost of Conducting Elections* (2022), Charles Stewart observes that voter services are different across the nation.

> Some states and localities flood mailboxes with voter guides, use the most up-to-date equipment, and deliver information and services on sophisticated websites. Others provide only minimal services to voters, rely on voters to figure out the details of voting on their own, and use equipment that is no longer manufactured or is incapable of being updated with the latest security patches (page 1).

All of these additional services add cost to election administration. So, how do our data on cost comport with observations about the significant differences in election administration across the country? In short, our data on the cost of election administration verifies that there are large and important differences across jurisdictions and over time.

This section describes the election administration cost data both geographically and over the period 2008–2016. Not surprisingly, we find that there is variation in funding across the nation. We describe patterns in spending that show the effects of the Great Recession, and uncover trends in spending at a regional level. By examining the data both across jurisdictions and over time, we also point out many features of the data that are important for the reader to understand when considering how time and geography affect spending. These descriptive analyses allow us to point to some of the limitations of the data and the nuances of local election administration in the United States.[34]

We first present the distribution of costs at the national level – between the states – and then, at the state level – between the counties and townships within a state. There is extreme variation between the states on expenditures. In some states like Florida and California, the spending is much higher than a state such as Vermont or Kentucky. There are many reasons for these differences in cost that go well beyond the general cost of living.

Secondly, we examine how costs have changed over time. The temporal component is relevant because the local jurisdictions that conduct elections have limited tax bases and competing services that they have to fund, such as streets, education, or public safety (McGowan et al., 2021). Therefore, the cost

---

[34] See Section 1 on the nature of these data and the unique challenge of measuring the costs of election administration in these states. We, therefore, present the data for forty-eight out of the fifty states.

of election administration has not stayed constant over the time period we analyze, which included the Great Recession (December 2007–June 2009).

Third, we examine how the costs have changed in different regions. Differences in how election jurisdictions responded to the Great Recession may have influenced how much they were and are currently spending on election administration. Also, changes over time to election methods are likely driving down costs in some regions – many western states, for example, have adopted voting-by-mail, which some reports say is cheaper to administer (Lamb, 2021). Others have adopted voting centers, where all precincts in a county are consolidated to (a) super-center(s) where any resident can vote. Such plans can reduce rent paid and staffing for multiple polling places spread throughout a jurisdiction (NCSL, 2023; Stein and Vonnahme, 2012).[35]

Finally, we discuss the county level of spending as an indication of within-state variation. Our dataset includes noncounty jurisdictions, like townships in New England, but examining the counties gives us insights into how much election spending varies within states. Some high-spending counties in low-spending states may actually spend more per voter than some of the low-spending counties in high-spending states. We discuss the reasons that we observe for this high amount of within-state variation.

National and State Level of Analysis

First, we examine the state-to-state variation in the average cost of election administration to see how much the cost of election administration varies across the country. Figure 1a provides a choropleth map of the real cost per registered voter in the states. We see significant state-to-state variation, with some of the highest costs per registered voter states being Florida and California (Figure 1b). As we will discuss in the individual state sections, these states have very different trends in their costs over the period, but overall these states spend significantly more on average than other states. In real dollars,[36] Florida spends $19.87 per registered voter on average and California spends $18.58. Other top spenders include New York and New Hampshire ($16.91 and $17.13 per registered voter, respectively).

---

[35] More recently, some have suggested that they may also increase costs if the services are too duplicative. While the current literature strongly suggests that vote centers reduce expenditure, this may in fact be an open question that could be tested with the data.

[36] We adjust the dollars to be constant 2020 dollars using the CPI-U series accounting for the fiscal year using the fiscal year end month (see McCulloch, 2022). "INFLATE: Stata module to inflate variables to real dollars using the CPI-U series," Statistical Software Components S459037, Boston College Department of Economics.

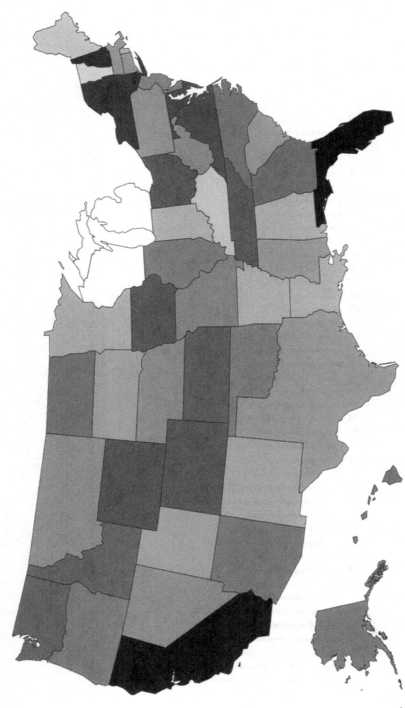

Figure 1a Map of election administration expenditure per registered voter in US states 2008–2016 (constant 2020 dollars)

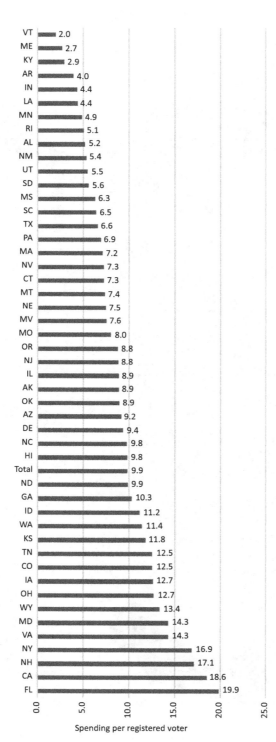

Figure 1b Graph of election administration expenditure per registered voter in US states 2008–2016 (constant 2020 dollars)

The low-spending states include states in New England and the South. As we may expect with the New England states with their traditional town hall style elections and historically frugal ways[37], these are some of the lowest cost-per-voter states. Vermont is the lowest at $2.04 per registered voter. Maine is the second lowest cost over the time period at $2.69 per registered voter and Kentucky is similarly thrifty at $2.95 per registered voter. Both the New England states and the Southern states are relatively sparsely populated. However, as we will see in the analysis of individual states and in Section 3, election administration costs are high in election jurisdictions that are sparsely populated because the fixed costs of election administration (election offices, voting machines) are higher as a proportion of total costs. Thus, the cost per voter tends to be higher in more sparsely populated areas. However, this may be offset by lower interest in funding election administration and government services. It is also the case that these low-cost states are also some of the most difficult to collect local financial data due to the very small governments and difficulty of accessing some of these reports. The small local governments are also much more likely to use a general county or village clerk as the election administrator, which means that they do not always classify the expenditures made for the clerk's time as an election administration cost. Especially during nonelection years, clerks may not report the ongoing cost of election adminis-tration activities – that is, updating voter rolls and routine maintenance and reporting. Therefore, these states on the lower end of spending should be treated with caution and recognize that they likely do not completely capture the total spending.[38]

In the middle of the distribution are the states from North Dakota, $9.89 per registered voter to Alaska at $8.92 per registered voter. These states include North Dakota, Hawaii, North Carolina, Delaware, Illinois, Arizona, Oklahoma, Oregon, and Alaska. These states are diverse in their election administration practices with Alaska and Delaware being the only states conducting election administration at the state level. North Dakota is the only state that conducts elections only in the even years largely through the county clerk's office and also it is the only state in the union without voter registration. North Carolina, in contrast, requires full-time elections administrators in every county above 6,500 people, which is almost all of them, and most counties conduct elections just

---

[37] For example, Vermont is the only state in the United States that does not require a balanced budget for its localities. This only works in practice because the culture is one of extreme frugality.

[38] This is another reason why we say that our estimates of the cost of election administration are a lower-bound estimate. We encourage more research to estimate how much of the cost is not accounted for in the financial statements. We discuss this further in the conclusion.

about every year. Oregon of course conducts its elections by mail. In short, the middle of the distribution is diverse in terms of its geography and its election administration practices. Therefore, we suggest the biggest driver of election administration costs from state to state is the local culture and practices of the state toward election administration and the appropriate level of funding for that administration.

Cost per Registered Voter versus Cost per Ballot Cast

Up to now, we have mostly been referring to the amount spent "per registered voter." In this section, we introduce a second way of standardizing the data: using cost per ballot cast. In terms of comparing the two measures of cost, the cost per ballot is usually higher because there are fewer people that cast ballots relative to the number of people that are registered to vote. We track the cost per ballot cast as an alternative measure of cost due to concerns that some states may be reducing voter rolls more aggressively than other states, which may inflate the estimate of spending over time due to a smaller denominator. Generally, we find that the trends that we report are the same for cost per registered voter and cost per ballot cast. An exception is interesting: In nonpresidential, federal election years, we almost always have a higher cost per ballot cast relative to the presidential election years where the denominator of ballots cast is much greater than nonpresidential years. We note the differences and in some cases similarities where it may be important. However, the rest of the analysis focuses on the cost per registered voter as the trend is more stable and straightforward to interpret due to the noncomplicating factor of voter turnout.

Election Spending across Time: 2008–2016

Timing in terms of year matters to the amount spent on elections, and not just because we have federal elections in even-numbered years. In this section, we consider both cost per registered voter and cost per ballot cast because they are different in terms of timing.[39] One thing to notice here is that when examining the spending per ballot, we can more clearly see the effects of the Great Recession on spending.

First, we examine spending per registered voter over time. Of course, election administration expenditures go down in the odd years that do not feature federal elections (see Figure 2). The cost of printing and staffing during these years decreases but does not disappear completely. This is because many election administrators conduct local elections in off years (the exception is North

---

[39] In this section, since we do not have the data from local elections, we use the number of ballots from the most recent federal election in nonfederal election years.

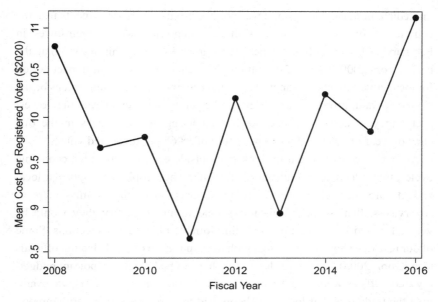

Figure 2 Election administration expenditure per registered voter from 2008 to 2016 (constant 2020 dollar)

Dakota), and there are a variety of election administration activities that must take place throughout the year and in the off years such as maintaining the poll records and election equipment. Over the period, the costs are the highest in the presidential election years of 2008, 2012, and 2016. The highest spending year is 2016 with $11.12 being spent per registered voter across the entire dataset for election administration in that year.

Although we will examine this in more detail in Section 3, you can visually see the impact of the Great Recession on the spending for election administration. The years following the Great Recession were some of the hardest years for local governments in the United States as the impact of the housing bubble was felt gradually by local governments as housing prices slowly reduced over time and resulted in lower property tax returns for the government, which is a major source of revenue for local governments. This impact of the Great Recession was not felt immediately by local governments. First, local government budgets are created a year in advance. So, the spending for the 2008 election would have been determined in 2007. Second, most local governments rely on property tax and did not feel the impact of the housing bubble right away. People are typically loss-averse and tend to hold onto their property even as the value continued to go down. However, as property values went down, local assessors had to adjust the value of the property down, but reassessments are not immediate in most places. So, it was not uncommon for reassessments in some counties to come a couple of years after housing prices were at their lowest in February 2012, according to the Case-Shiller Index.[40] This means that the period from 2009 to about 2013 should be seen as the recession-impact period for local governments (Mohr et al., 2020). After this time, housing values began to go up and property tax revenues began to recover. Thus, the lowest spending year according to expenditure per registered voter is in the off-election year of 2011 with an expenditure of $8.65 per registered voter.

At first it seems unusual to think that outside events such as the economic cycle affect election administration funding. The people who approve local budgets are themselves elected (often a local board of commissioners or supervisors, that is, local legislators). One would think that they would be very interested in having high spending to have high-quality elections. Some of our research shows – consistent with the experience of local election officials (see Kropf, 2005) – that local legislators have to make other important budgetary trade-offs as well. In our past research (McGowan et al., 2021), we examined the trade-offs that local legislators had to make regarding very common and very visible local services such as education and public safety. These things are highly visible, and unlike elections, most people pay attention to them every single year, or more accurately, every single day. Election administration is not visible for most constituents except in national election years. This may influence the trade-offs toward more immediate priorities like roads, public schools, or public safety (McGowan et al., 2021). For example, former Boone County, Missouri County Clerk Wendy Noren noted in 2003, "I've got county commissioners that don't mind spending 1 million dollars on a road that will serve 1,000 people. But the thought of needing a million dollars for election equipment that'll serve 60,000 people is just beyond comprehension to them."[41]

In Figure 3, we examine spending per ballot cast. In spite of the dip following the recession, the expenditure per registered voter starts to rise after 2013. As housing prices and tax collections increased, the ability for local government to spend more returned. We also see a clear upward trend when we observe the cost per ballot cast. The highest spending year in terms of ballots cast is nonpresidential election year is 2014 – when there was relatively high spending and unusually low voter turnout. The lowest spending year in terms of ballots cast is 2013. In terms of comparing the two measures of cost, the cost per ballot cast is usually higher because there are fewer people that vote relative to the number of people that are registered to vote.

---

[40] https://fred.stlouisfed.org/series/CSUSHPINSA, last accessed August 1, 2023.
[41] Wendy Noren Interview with Martha Kropf, April 16, 2003, Columbia, Missouri.

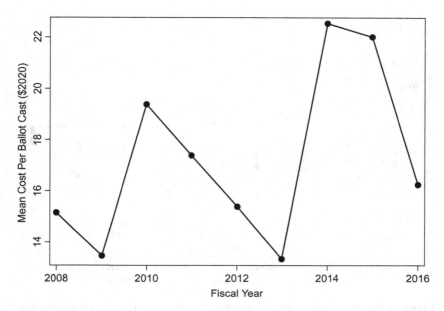

Figure 3 Election administration expenditure per ballot cast from 2008 to 2016 (constant 2020 dollar)

Regional Analysis

The trend in spending per registered voter (Figure 2) showed that there was a dip following the 2008 election that is likely due to the recession and the housing value lag in the years following. Only by the 2016 election had the spending recovered to the point that it was more than in 2008 when adjusted for inflation. While this is an intuitive and compelling story, the different regions of the country responded to the recession and the years following the recession in very different ways. There have also been major changes to election technology and election methods in different regions that make exploring the trends in spending by region quite compelling.

Figure 4, which shows the trends over time by the different regions, shows the regions have very different trends in spending. For example, the South shows robust growth in spending over time. The southern region starts out with the lowest spending in 2008 of $9.11 per registered voter. By 2016, the cost per registered voter had increased to $11.00, which is more than that spent in the Midwest in 2016. Like the other regions, the South hit its lowest spending during the years following the recession. In 2010, that spending bottomed out at $8.55 per registered voter, but then it experienced a strong increase making it the region with the largest growth in election administration spending – an increase of 20.80 percent in real spending per registered voter.

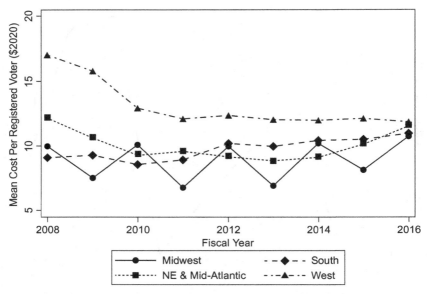

Figure 4 Election administration expenditure per registered voter from 2008 to 2016 by region (constant 2020 dollar)

Why this increasing trend for spending on election administration in the South when two of the other regions experienced lower spending over this time is still unknown at this point. We have two observations about this period for the South. First, the South has experienced tremendous domestic migration during this period. More people and increased building of housing and businesses means that the tax base is larger, which frees up spending for things such as election administration. Second, the migrants to places such as North Carolina, Tennessee, Georgia, and Florida are mostly coming from the Northeast and Mid-Atlantic region where the spending is much higher. We suspect that they bring their expectations for elections with them.[42] More money and higher expectations are a likely recipe for greater spending on election administration.

The Northeast and Mid-Atlantic region has a similar trend in spending as the nation as a whole over the period. However, unlike the total spending shown in Figure 2, the Northeast and Mid-Atlantic region ends up spending less in 2016 per registered voter than it spent in 2008. This region in 2008 spent $12.15 per registered voter. By 2016, the spending per registered voter had decreased to $11.54, which is only slightly more than that spent by the South in

---

[42] It is also true that the South started out from the lowest spending level, which means that a modest increase in spending will appear to be a large increase in percentage terms.

2016. The spending decreases much more and for longer in the Northeast and Mid-Atlantic than in the South, for example. The lowest level of spending in the Northeast and Mid-Atlantic was $8.81 per registered voter in 2013. It does start to recover after that point with increases every year to 2016. However, the net change from 2008 to 2016 is a decrease in spending of five percent in real expenditure per registered voter.

The reasons for this change in the Northeast and Mid-Atlantic are also not well known, but we suspect that the story for this region is the opposite than that of the South. Migration out of large cities and the region to places in the South and West may have put pressure to decrease spending for all goods and services provided by local government, which may include election administration. Also, changes in election technology and learning to use the technology may be making this region more similar to other regions. As the region started out with a relatively high cost of election administration, the cost may be declining due to increasing efficiency and policy learning. In fact, one of the most interesting things about this graph is the seeming convergence in the cost of election administration across the four regions. It will be interesting to see if the regions continue to converge on a similar level of spending, or if they change due to differences in demand for election administration and due to differences in voting technology and methods.

Perhaps even more impressive than the South's growth in spending on election administration is the sustained decrease in spending in the West region. The West region begins in 2008 with the highest level of spending at $17.15 per registered voter. By 2016, the spending per registered voter had decreased to $11.77, which is only slightly more than that spent by the Northeast and Mid-Atlantic in 2016. The spending decreases from 2008 to 2016, which is a bit shocking but also perhaps not unexpected. The spending in the West in 2016 is $11.77 per registered voter. This is a decrease in spending of over 31 percent.

We suspect that part of the story in the West is like the Northeast and Mid-Atlantic, but it also is significantly different from that region. Following the Great Recession, the West experienced some of the highest fiscal stress from the loss of housing values and other financial decisions made before the Great Recession. The other very interesting possibility is that the West has made substantial changes to its voting systems with many states encouraging the use of mail voting. Experts note that mail voting should have a lower cost due to use of fewer vote counting machines and the need for less staffing. Unfortunately, we do not have very complete data for states such as Oregon that have gone to all mail voting. Another potential hypothesis concerning the drop in expenditures in the West is the increasing use of vote centers on Election Day during the time period we analyze. According to the National Conference of State

Legislatures, several states began implementing vote centers: Arizona (2011), Colorado (2004), New Mexico (2011), Utah (2011), Washington (2011), and Wyoming (2015).[43] Many of these same states (since we have worked on this research) have implemented vote-by-mail (Kropf, 2024). We do not test either hypothesis here, but analyses in other countries and in Colorado suggest that methods of voting that do not require people to go to the polls may have much lower costs.[44]

The Midwest region does not have a strong change from 2008 to 2016 like the other regions, but that does not mean that it is unimportant or that we cannot learn something from examining the trends in the region. In 2008, the Midwest spent $9.98 per registered voters and by 2016 that amount had climbed to $10.74, which is a modest increase in spending of 7.61 percent. Like both the South and the Northeast and Mid-Atlantic regions, the spending in the Midwest bottoms out after the Great Recession in 2011 at $6.79. One reason that the Midwest may have stayed reasonably strong during this time period is that there has not been as much population change as the other regions and the value of farmland has stayed strong during the period.

Perhaps the most interesting thing about the Midwest is the cyclical variation from federal election years (even numbered years) and the local election years (odd numbered years). All jurisdictions have higher costs in federal election years as the cost for printing, staffing, and generally all things that vary by the number of voters increase during federal election years. We see some fluctuation in cost in all states and all regions during federal election years and local election years: however, the trend is much more pronounced in the Midwest. The reason for this is likely who conducts the elections in the Midwest. In less populated places such as most of the counties in the Midwest, the county clerk is responsible for election administration and likely does not have a dedicated staff for elections as some clerks in larger jurisdictions have. For the recording of election costs during the federal election years this means the clerk is much more aware of the time that they and their staff put into election administration. They might record a portion of that time as election administration or maybe

---

[43] According to the NCSL (2024), other states have also established vote centers during our study period: Arkansas (2013), Indiana (2006), Iowa ("for some elections," 2008), North Dakota (2007), South Dakota (2012), Tennessee (2008), and Texas (2009).

[44] We spoke to several California election officials at the 8th Annual Election Science, Reform, and Administration Conference in Los Angeles (2024) who suggested the cost of vote centers (established in 2017) was greater for them than traditional polling places. While we do not test the impact of different forms of voting on cost here, we expect that researchers will make use of these data to do so. As we discuss in the Conclusion, there also needs to be a sustained research program that analyzes the disaggregated cost of election administration so that scholars can measure the cost of different voting methods, especially within election jurisdictions that offer multiple forms of voting.

they have a part-time staff person during those election years. However, in the local election years, the clerk may spend some time doing things such as maintaining the election rolls and/or routine standard reporting, but they may not record these as separate costs relative to their nonelection duties.

While the story over time for the nation as a whole is that of responding to the Great Recession, expenditures on election administration in the different regions responded very differently. These differences in election spending are worth observing in the time period after 2016. We predict we will see changes in election forms impact election administration spending. In particular, COVID-19 is an exogenous shock that affected all the regions on shifting forms of elections, meaning that costs are likely affected and affected by the pure effect of changing election form and not the need to respond to some external fiscal pressure.

County Analysis

In this county-level descriptive analysis, we present a map of the data that shows larger dots where the election jurisdictions spend more (Figure 5). Since the larger dots represent higher levels of spending, it is not at all surprising that states like California, New York, and Florida have some of the highest spending counties. However, one can see that even in these states there are some counties that do not spend very much. For example, San Bernadino, the very large county to the west of LA, does not spend nearly as much as most other California counties. So, the counties have very high levels of variation in how much they spend. For example, we would expect that two counties in North Carolina that are side by side and have very similar populations in terms of demographics (age, race, education, etc.) would spend about the same amount. However, we found several examples of very different levels of spending by similar counties in North Carolina. For example, in southeast North Carolina, we found that one county was spending about $8 per voter and an adjacent county was spending about $12 per voter, which is nearly 50 percent more spent on election administration.[45]

In the North Carolina case, we found that a big part of the story was politics and the interaction of politics and elected officials. In a previously published study, we found that Republican County Commissions spent less on elections only when the county was likely to vote Republican (Mohr et al., 2019). Why there is an interactive relationship between the partisanship of the County Commission, which sets the election administration budget, and the partisanship of the county

---

[45] We provide a very preliminary analysis in Section 3 using the forty-eight-state dataset, but a definitive answer will also take much more analysis. We do not have the partisan variables at the election jurisdiction level or all of the controls that would be needed for an analysis like we are describing in North Carolina.

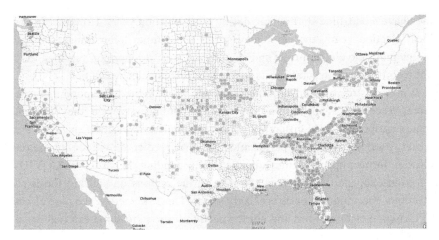

Figure 5 County election spending per registered voter in the dataset
(constant 2020 dollar)

voters is not completely known. However, the data are consistent with two theories
that we argue explain this difference in the level of spending. First, political
science research (DeNardo, 1980; Gomez et al., 2007) discusses how core and
peripheral voters behave differently. Particularly, peripheral voters may be more
erratic and less likely to vote for their party's candidate. Therefore, the Republican
County Commissions with an increasingly strong partisan advantage (and also
Democratic Commissions with their own partisan advantage) are likely to reduce
election spending as they approach and exceed a majority. The other reason that
politics is likely to strongly influence election spending is the effect of partisan
policy preferences. We see reasons for both parties to want more spending. As
a general rule, we have argued (McGowan et al., 2021) that Democrats would like
more government spending generally; however, Republicans may also have things
such as election security. They are very interested in funding in elections.
Therefore, it is not a straightforward story even in the same state or even in
neighboring counties with very similar demographic and social makeups.

However, the map reveals some compelling patterns. While some large cities
such as Chicago and Cook County spend much more than the smaller election
jurisdictions in their state, the general trend shows fairly high levels of spending
in the more rural counties. What explains this? If we suspect that demographics
such as education levels or Republican counties with lots of Republican voters
are the main driving force of election spending, then we would believe that these
counties should spend the least. However, we find that in places like rural
Kansas or rural Iowa, there are high levels of spending in many of the smallest

counties. In North Carolina, the highest levels of spending per voter are on the coasts or in the mountains. The main reason for this is that these smaller jurisdictions must spend more per voter because they have approximately the same amount of area to cover but many fewer people to spread the costs. In the parlance of economics, they have high fixed costs and fewer people, which means a high average cost per voter in these smaller, rural jurisdictions. Let us be clear, these jurisdictions are not spending more in total on election administration but $30,000 divided by 300 voters is more per voter than $5 million dollars spent on election administration for a million voters. So, election administration is not just about politics. Spatial distribution and microeconomic factors matter greatly to the cost of conducting election administration.[46]

The map also illustrates we have missing data, as we discussed in Section 1. Unfortunately, it was very hard to collect election costs in some of these jurisdictions. First, we had to get a financial report or a budget with actual levels of spending in it, and it is not surprising that the smaller jurisdictions were much less likely to post these on the internet.[47] The local jurisdictions then had to break out the cost for the election administration separately from general administration or the clerk. In very small jurisdictions, this is unlikely and may even vary considerably from year to year. So, in some of the very smallest jurisdictions and the states many very small jurisdictions are unlikely to have election cost data collected. We can see that states like Montana, New Mexico, Arkansas, Alabama, and Kentucky have very low levels of collection; in general, scholars relying on these data alone will not be able to make valid conclusions based on these data. This is why we focus on the states with very high levels of collection in Section 4 and we discuss our formal process for determining the states that are sufficiently collected in Section 1.

Conclusion

These analyses are descriptive in nature. However, we have seen that there is great variation between the states; costs range from just over $2 to almost $20 per voter, which is an order of magnitude that we think is compelling and worth investigating further, especially because we have long heard that voter services vary so much across the nation. The costs change over time, and these costs are not monotonically increasing. In fact, when we look at the different regions, we see very different patterns in election spending that are likely driven by demographic shifts, underlying financial resources, and changes in election

---

[46] We further discuss economies and dis-economies of scale in Section 3.
[47] Some of the smallest jurisdictions may not even be required to produce audited financial statements.

administration practice. Finally, when we look within states, we also see very large differences in the level of spending. We have only offered suggestions to this point at why the cost of election administration may be different, but in Section 3 we conduct inferential statistical analysis of some of the basic factors that may influence election costs.

3 What Affects How Much Is Spent on Election Administration?

In Section 2, we discussed how election administration costs differ throughout the country and over time. Macro level forces such as population shifts and changing preferences likely contribute to changes in the expenditures. However, election administration scholars have long known that there are also many factors that affect election costs such as voting modalities, the type of voting technology, and changes to technology (Hill, 2012). Characteristics of the jurisdiction such as average age and education level, among many others, also have effects on the amount spent on election administration (Mohr et al., 2019). Here, we tackle two of the technical issues that matter a great deal for setting the election budget and developing an appropriate level of spending: economies of scale and the impact of economic conditions.

First, we examine the effect of the size of the jurisdiction on election administration spending. A common election cost finding is the effect of economies of scale. While we want to confirm the economies of scale finding on these data, we also want to examine the effect of both a large amount of data and data from very large communities to see if there is a point at which economies of scale no longer apply. At a certain point, the organization of elections may become too large and complex, which leads to higher cost of providing election administration in very large jurisdictions. In economic terms, we test both economies and diseconomies of scale.

In the subsection Economies and Diseconomies of Scale, we test the effect of macroeconomic conditions on election spending similar to our analysis from four states (Mohr et al., 2020). We provide suggestive evidence in Section 2, but Mohr et al. (2020) provided evidence that economic conditions had a significant effect on lowering the amount of election administration spending both during the 2008–09 recession and the housing lag period after, which influenced property tax receipts significantly in the years following the recession. Using this national dataset, we extend our previous analyses and find that the impact of the recession may be even greater than previously discussed. This analysis shows that technical factors such as the economy can influence the amount of funds for elections. Local governments, who fund elections, experience hard constraints in the form of the local tax base on the amount they can spend for services.

We choose not to delve into demographic factors that influence expenditures in this Element. Rather, we make the choice to introduce these data to scholars and highlight some issues for consideration. Thus, in the conclusion to the section, we look ahead to what other analyses scholars might do with these data. We also discuss the limitations of the analysis of which people need to be aware when analyzing predictors of election administration cost. As elections change and additional expectations are added or subtracted from election administration, the cost of providing the service will change. Understanding what influences election costs becomes critically important for having data-informed policy discussions about election administration and election policy.

Economies and Diseconomies of Scale

As with practically any governmental or private business operation, the more things that you make or the more customers you serve, economies of scale tend to drive down the per unit cost. This is because there are always some fixed costs (such as the election office) and some variable costs (such as ballots) and the per unit proportion of the fixed cost becomes smaller as the output increases. This is standard microeconomic theory but what are the fixed costs that get spread out as election administration serves more voters? One example is the building space for election administration. The per voter cost for election administrators who are organizing an election for 100,000 voters is likely much less than the cost per voter for an election administrator who is serving only 1,000 voters. But we think there is a point at which the election administration operation becomes so large and so complex that the economies of scale no longer pertain and we need to hire more election administrators or rent more equipment and space. This is a diseconomy of scale and there are some statements in the literature that suggest that this might also be possible (Caltech–MIT Voting Technology Project, 2001). However, to this point, the election science community lacked the data to fully assess this because there are usually only a few very large cities in each state, and since the prior analyses examined only individual states, there were not enough observations of large jurisdictions.

Theoretically speaking, we could hypothesize that costs are linear – as the number of registered voters increases, cost decreases proportionately (economies of scale). Or, we could consider population as a squared term (nonlinear), where we hypothesize that cost decreases with increasing registered voters until a certain point, and then increases (in graph terms, the shape is a "u"). When we run the analysis predicting real cost per registered voter by jurisdiction size and

Table 3 Effect of jurisdiction size on election cost per registered voter

Variable	Coefficient (std. error)	
Registered voters (thousands)	−0.006796	***
	(0.0004)	
Registered voters (thousands)-squared	0.0000014	***
	(0.0000)	
Constant	7.6635	
	(0.6744)	
Sample size	16,832	
ICC – State	0.287 (0.0428)	***
Model fit	−55,874.798	

***p < 0.001; year fixed effected omitted

jurisdiction size squared (Table 3),[48] we can clearly see the nonlinear effect. First, the size of the jurisdiction term that is not squared is negative and strongly statistically significant (*p* < 0.001; Table 3). As we expect from economies of scale, larger jurisdictions do pay less per registered voter than the smallest jurisdictions (Figure 6). The model predicts – without taking into account the squared term – that as a jurisdiction gets larger (i.e., from 0 to 1,000 registered voters), the cost per voter will decrease by approximately 0.68 cents per registered voter.

However, this is not the whole story because the squared term is significant and predicts a nonlinear effect on costs. Looking at Figure 6, we see that jurisdictions get increasingly less economy of scale and the model predicts that elections cost much more per registered voter in the very largest jurisdictions. So, this is a practically and statistically large effect (*p* < 0.001) that shows that there are diseconomies of scale in the very largest jurisdictions.

While we do not have a causal test of why diseconomies of scale happen in large jurisdictions, we can make some observations from the literature and personal observations. First, scholars suspect that as governments get larger, they are less accountable and may not use their resources as efficiently as smaller governments. While this may be the case, we have not once talked to an election administrator who seemed to carelessly waste their resources. In fact, they tend to manage their budgets with care (Stewart, 2022). A second

---

[48] We control for year fixed effects and state random effects. We also ran it as a state and year fixed effects model and results are similar in terms of sign and statistical significance of the coefficients.

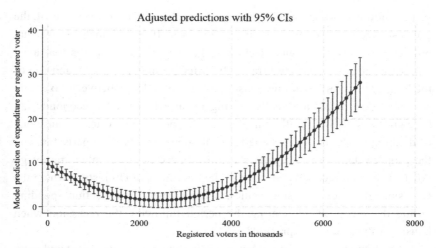

Figure 6 Effect of jurisdiction size on election administration expenditure (size in thousands)

possibility is that as the operation becomes larger, the complexity of the operation increases. The level of coordination that is needed in Los Angeles County (the largest jurisdiction with 6.7 million registered voters in 2016) is much greater than an average county like Putnam County, Tennessee (approximately 43,000 registered voters in 2016) needs and the complexity of serving a much more diverse metro area is also on a different order of magnitude. It is not surprising, then, that in 2016 Putnam County spent $9.13 per registered voter and LA county spent $16.31.[49] Finally, we would also note that states often instruct the largest jurisdictions to do additional activities that small jurisdictions do not have to do. For example, Denver County is the largest county in Colorado and has additional duties such as keeping track of campaign finance filings. The other counties in Colorado do not have to do this activity and so it should not be a surprise that these largest counties also have a broader scope of work than do many of the smaller counties.

The Effect of the Economy on Election Cost

When we first started talking with political scientists about the cost of election administration, one of the questions we always got was "Why wouldn't local politicians fully fund election administration?" The logic

---

[49] Amounts in real dollars. Also, it should be noted that other large jurisdictions like New York spent more than LA county. The model is an average effect from registered voters and registered voters squared, and the confidence intervals become quite large at the very highest ends of the model.

from a political perspective was sound. Local politicians are some of the savviest election experts in their jurisdictions. It would make sense that politicians would fully fund elections. The problem of course is that local politicians also make difficult trade-offs (McGowan et al., 2021), and one of the biggest trade-offs that they must make is the trade-off between taxes and spending. Are politicians really willing to raise taxes if the economic tax base goes down? Thankfully, this does not happen all that often because one of the biggest sources of revenue for local governments is property tax, and the property tax base rarely goes down because housing values rarely go down. The 2008 recession was one of the rare times in US history where the recession influenced housing values. What happened to election spending during the recession and during the period following the recession when housing values stayed depressed?

As we descriptively discuss in Section 2, the expenditure per registered voter did decrease significantly following the recession and stayed depressed until the 2016 presidential election. We tested the effect of economic conditions in earlier research (Mohr et al., 2020) that examined the effect of the economic cycle in four states: Ohio, New Jersey, North Carolina, and Georgia. We found election spending did go down during the recessionary period (2008–09) and in the housing lag period (2010–12) relative to the prerecessionary period (2005–07). In that analysis, we found expenditures had recovered for these four states by the postrecessionary period (2013–16). What we did not fully appreciate at that time was how different the different regions of the country were and how they responded differently in terms of election spending from 2008 to 2016. Given that half of the states (North Carolina and Georgia) were in the South that has exhibited strong expenditure growth for election administration, the finding that the postrecessionary period had recovered relative to the prerecessionary period is perhaps being driven by these states.

In fact, when we go back and study election administration expenditures for these four periods, we find that the earlier research understated the effect of economic conditions after the Great Recession on election administration funding (Table 4; Model 1).[50] We see that on the full dataset (forty-eight states), in the postrecessionary period (2013–16), expenditures had not fully recovered. Model 1 shows that spending relative to the prerecessionary period was $0.49 per registered voter less during the recessionary period, $1.13 per registered voter less during the housing lag period, and $.78 less during the postrecessionary period. This means that expenditures during the postrecessionary period had started to recover relative to the lowest points during the

---

Table 4 Effect of economic condition on election administration expenditures

Economic period	Model 1 coefficient (std. error)	Model 2 coefficient (std. error)
Recessionary	−0.491*	-
	(0.227)	-
Housing lag	−1.130**	−0.638**
	(0.253)	(0.118)
Postrecessionary	−0.776**	−0.285
	(0.279)	(0.169)
Constant	10.70**	10.21**
	(0.285)	(0.189)
Observations	16,836	14,851
R-squared	0.002	0.001

Robust standard errors in parentheses
**$p < 0.01$, *$p < 0.05$

housing lag period, but it had not fully recovered relative to the prerecessionary levels. If you review Figure 2, you see that in terms of cost per registered voter in 2013 was almost as bad nationally as 2011 at the depths of the housing lag. It really was not until 2016 that the spending on election administration started to exceed the expenditure in 2008.

Examining these data again, we make two important caveats about the data during the 2005–16 period.[51] First, it may be somewhat doubtful whether the 2008 spending was in a recessionary period. The reason for this is that the budgets for FY 2008 are made in 2007. The spending for 2008 might still be strong even though we see a negative effect in the model for the recessionary period. However, we suspect that budgeters were perhaps taking into account worsening fiscal conditions even in 2007, and the spending that we are actually observing may be cut even after the budget is made. So, if financial conditions were bad (and they very much were in some places in 2008), then the spending could be cut relative to their original budget amount. Second, in looking at the trends over a longer period (2005–16), we also see large spending in 2005 and 2006 as local governments made equipment purchases with their HAVA funds.

---

[51] We use 2005 because it comports with our earlier analysis and the period 2005–2008 is the baseline in the regression. Because we have argued that the pre-2008 period might be contaminated by HAVA spending – in fact it likely was – we then run the analysis in Model 2 with the recessionary period as the baseline in the regression. Either way shows that economic periods have an impact on the election spending.

Because of the cash and modified accrual accounting that is used in local governments, these purchases are seen as large increases in expenditures.[52] So, a more conservative model of the effect of economic conditions would be to look at the housing lag period and the postrecessionary period relative to the recessionary period. We do this in Table 4, Model 2. We find that the housing lag period has significantly lower expenditure relative to the recessionary period but the postrecessionary period is not significantly different from the recessionary period. Our point with Model 2 is that even a more "conservative" test indicates the economic condition is influencing the amount spent on election administration.

Conclusion

The findings from this analysis of the factors that affect election administration cost advance our understanding in two important ways. First, there are economies of scale, but the very largest jurisdictions spend more per voter as size increases. This may be because of diseconomies of scale caused by complexity, coordination, and accountability problems. It may also be caused by states increasing the scope of operations for large jurisdictions. Second, economic conditions strongly influence election administration spending. In fact, the impact of the Great Recession on election administration spending may be even more pronounced and last for longer than previously recognized.

We recognize that these analyses do not include partisanship and race, among other potential variables to explain spending. We do not do so for two main reasons. First, these data are incomplete. We show in Section 1 that these data are not missing randomly – whether we have "cost" is related to the size of the jurisdiction.[53] We also note that for some of our counties, the data represent a lower-bound estimate of costs as discussed in Section 1. Therefore, we are concerned that nationwide analyses might present a biased picture of the problems within election administration today.

Second, this Element is about introducing the data and starting the conversation about whether election officials can credibly run our republic on current funding levels, and not introducing a polarized debate about overt partisanship or racism. Especially for controversial concepts such as race and partisanship,

---

[52] This is another reason that we focus throughout this Element on the period after 2008. At this point, most of the money from the 2002 HAVA grant should have been spent.

[53] It is important to note that the costs of elections are not random. We have done some preliminary analysis of some of the social determinants of election cost and they are significantly related in some of the analyses. However, they may not be when we look at the significantly collected states or when we are able to control for other important third variables. Thus, it is important to understand the limitations of the data, which we describe further in the conclusion.

we did not feel it appropriate to model these variables. We think that would muddy the discussion and the most important idea we present: The amount spent on democracy depends on where you live. We show in the next section that the amount spent on election administration has implications for public confidence in elections – we do so using the states for which we have the most complete data.

We hope that scholars will do additional research with these data. Ideally, we would encourage scholars to examine one or a couple of more complete states in order to learn about how costs are related to these all-important political variables, following our lead in the next section to limit the analysis to states where the data are most complete.

4 Election Administration Expenditures and Election/Voter Outcomes

In this Element, the analyses up to now focus on explaining the level of expenditures among jurisdictions for which we have data. Our data show that the amount localities spend on elections varies widely among jurisdictions. We hope we add to the conversation about whether election spending is adequate, even if we do not completely answer that question. These data allow us to consider the important research question about what the effects are of differing levels of election spending on election "outcomes" such as voter perceptions and experience.

Thus, in this section, first we examine whether expenditures explain variables related to voters such as perceptions of fraud and voter confidence; we also argue these attitudes measure "procedural legitimacy." Then we look at five variables measuring voter experiences at the polls. These include pollworker performance, operations at the polling place, wait time/line length, voter registration, and voting equipment. These voter process variables likely have a direct effect on voter confidence. We check to see if expenditures matter to these outcomes even when considering the election jurisdiction size, and various respondent-level factors such as the winner's effect, race, education, and income. This section begins with a discussion of voter confidence and perceptions about whether voter fraud exists using public opinion data from the Survey of the Performance of American Elections (SPAE) (Stewart, 2013a, 2013b, 2017).[54] We combine these data with our election administration expenditure data in our analysis at the end of the sub section. Next, we discuss the relationship between the expenditures and the voting process outcomes. We then theoretically discuss that there are some factors that voters may *not* be able to observe. These include administrative rules followed by

---

[54] The SPAE has continued on in 2020 and 2022, and will continue into 2024.

election administrators or some important aspects of the polling places. We expect these factors that citizens may not observe to lead to a relationship between election administration spending and outcomes that is likely to be nonlinear.

As Section 1 discussed, we examine this relationship among the nine states for which we have complete or nearly complete data that have passed a nonresponse analysis.[55] These analyses show the complex but important relationship between election administration expenditures and voter outcomes. We conclude this section with a discussion of the implication that much of what is "purchased" by more resources for elections administration may not be observable to voters and the limitations of our analysis.

Election Spending and Evaluations of Elections

The question of "do resources matter?" is a surprisingly vexing one for social scientists in many policy areas. Studies of the relationship between budgeted resources and government outcomes, the relationship is often not a direct, linear relationship. In examining services such as education, the locations that have the greatest need and the worst outcomes are some of the most expensive to serve. So, there is an observed inverse relationship or no observable relationship as the effect of more resources is offset by greater need and often lower outcomes (e.g., Hanushek, 1997; see also Pressman and Wildavsky, 1984).

In election administration, scholars have examined the connection between financial resources and problems with voting through measures such as the residual vote rate (Kropf et al., 2020) and turnout (Burden and Neiheisel, 2013; Kropf and Pope, 2020), but these studies are of single states. Furthermore, Kropf and colleagues did not find a relationship between the election expenditures and residual votes; rather, they found that greater administrative capacity as measured by more highly paid election directors is associated with a lower residual vote rate (Kropf et al., 2020).

This analysis looks at how expenditures affect specific outcomes of elections, including voters' perceptions of confidence their ballot was counted, the public perceptions of fraud, and the voting process or voter experience. We utilize five "voter experience" questions on the SPAE that scholars associate with voter confidence. We analyze whether expenditures affect these voter experience variables. We also consider the idea that spending may lead to confidence

---

[55] As noted in Section 1, as a check to make sure we had the same results, we also analyzed the effects of election expenditures using four additional states which passed the nonresponse analysis for a limited number of years, so we only used those years: Delaware (2008, 2012), Florida (2012, 2016), Indiana (2012, 2016), and North Carolina (2008, 2012). We conduct this robustness check because the nine states do not include any states from the South. The results are largely the same as that reported in this section.

because of factors the voters might observe (wait times, voting equipment, registration, polling place operations, and poll workers). Finally, we expect there are things that election officials do that voters never see (polling place quality, voter education, how well elections follow administrative rules), but nevertheless may lead to higher levels of confidence. We develop our theoretical expectations here.

Public Opinion Toward Elections: Confidence

One basic input of our democratic system is whether public opinion supports the system. Political scientist Paul Gronke (2014, p. 251) writes that voter confidence is "trust or faith in the political system." At least since the 2000 election, scholars have examined voter confidence as a key metric or performance measure in judging the quality of elections within states (Atkeson, 2011; Atkeson, 2014; Atkeson et al., 2015; Bryant, 2020; Gronke, 2014). Voter confidence, therefore, focuses on the *process* of democracy that is, voting, rather than on the governmental system more generally or on political leaders. In other words, it measures beliefs in "procedural legitimacy." If a citizen does not believe the elections to be fair and accurate – starting with their vote – then it is difficult for them to support the government and obey the laws that the government created (Tyler, 2006). Atkeson (2011, p. 6) adds, "if citizens do not believe in the election process, then the entire system of republican government becomes a questionable enterprise." The idea of public confidence in elections became the legal basis for the 2008 Supreme Court decision in *Crawford* v. *Marion County*. The Court ruled in *Crawford* v. *Marion County* (2008) that "public confidence in the integrity of the electoral process has independent significance, because it encourages citizen participation in the democratic process."

Voter Confidence Measurement. A number of surveys have measured "confidence" (Sances and Stewart, 2015), but the Survey of the Performance of American Elections (SPAE; Stewart, 2013a, 2013b, 2017) is a long-running postelection survey that asks questions specifically about the voting experience, including voter confidence. Questions are largely similar over time, including the question, "How confident are you that *your vote* in the General Election was counted as you intended?" Yet, this way of measuring "voter confidence" suffers from a noticeable skewness in distribution in a variety of surveys. Often when considering whether their own ballot is counted, the vast majority of voters give positive responses (see Figure 7).

Aside from its skewed nature, Gronke (2014) notes the measure is subject to a winner's effect – a voter is significantly more confident their own ballot is

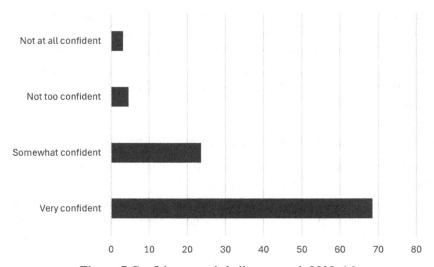

Figure 7 Confidence one's ballot counted, 2008–16
(**Source**: SPAE, 2008–2016 pooled; weighted frequencies, *nine states*)[56]

counted if their party wins the election, which many scholars have confirmed (e.g., Sances and Stewart, 2015; Sinclair et al., 2019; Stewart et al., 2016). Yet, he concludes: "In short, while it is undoubtedly true that voter confidence is a subjective measure, it responds in reasonable ways to reasonable features of the election system and to characteristics and perceptions [on the part of the voter] of the officials who administer the system." He further concludes: "It is far from an incoherent jumble of emotions or short-term reactions" (page 266). Given the measure's strong use and conceptualization as a measure that indicates a belief in procedural legitimacy, we argue that the idea of "confidence in elections" is well-justified as a dependent variable to allow us to examine how money affects election outputs. Using the SPAE survey from the years 2008, 2012, and 2016, we can see whether there are changes in voter confidence with differences in levels of expenditures.[57] Adding our expenditure data into the survey database (connecting counties in the SPAE data to counties in the expenditure data), we can test how the amount spent per registered voter affects confidence. To account for the "winner's effect" we create a variable in the analysis to indicate whether the individual in the survey's party won the presidential election.

---

[56] Responses of "Not sure" are removed from this analysis.

[57] The 2012–2016 surveys ask about the voters' confidence in county, state, and national elections, but to maximize the time frame, we examine only voters' confidence that their own ballot was counted as cast (see Sances and Stewart, 2015 for a discussion of egotropic versus sociotropic voter confidence).

Public Opinion Toward Elections: Belief in the Existence of Fraud

Closely tied to confidence in whether one's vote is counted is how much election fraud one believes there is. This part of the discussion is not about the actual existence of fraud – most scholars say there is very little evidence of fraud – but rather about how people view the possibility of fraud. According to political scientists Charles Stewart III and Stephen Ansolabehere and law professor Nathaniel Persily, the perception of fraud is behind much of the court's reasons supporting voter identification laws (2016). They write that voter identification laws "would do so by convincing voters that, whatever the reality, such laws decrease voter fraud at the polls" (page 1457). Examining the SPAE fraud questions, Stewart and colleagues find that the questions about fraud are closely related to each other – that is, survey respondents provide similar answers to different questions about fraud.

> This high intercorrelation suggests that beliefs about fraud derive from a single underlying attitude about the fairness of elections and, quite likely, about generalized trust in government itself. In other words, despite the fact that the legal- and election-administration communities make fine distinctions between the sources of election fraud, survey respondents who see one type of fraud as prevalent tend to see other types of fraud as prevalent as well. (page 1469)

Together with confidence that one's vote is counted as cast, a belief about the existence of fraud may indicate a citizen's belief in the fairness and accuracy of the electoral system. The use of a fraud variable is not as broadly accepted a measure of support for the voting experience as the confidence measure. Regardless, the fraud variable can give us more assurance that we are analyzing how expenditures affect perceptions of belief in procedural legitimacy. Along with Stewart and colleagues (2016), political scientist Lonna Atkeson (2014) shows that perceptions of fraud strongly affect the level of voter confidence. Furthermore, Gronke shows that "perceptions of voter fraud are a powerful force, ranking as one of the most important determinants of voter confidence" (2014, p. 267). Similarly, as suggested, there is a winner's effect – winners perceive that there is less election fraud. Belief in fraud is also highly skewed toward respondents reporting that fraud is very common (see Figures 8 and 9).

Voter Belief in Fraud Measurement. How do scholars measure how much voter fraud the public believes there is? Again, we turn to the SPAE, which asks about perceptions of fraud. Note that the survey asks about fraud perceptions slightly differently in 2008 than in 2012 and 2016. Two questions from 2008 and two questions from 2012 to 2016 are comparable, though asked slightly differently, allowing us to cover the

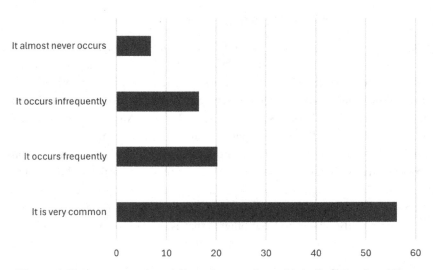

Figure 8 How common is stealing or tampering with ballots that have been voted? 2008–16
(**Source**: SPAE, 2008–2016 pooled; weighted frequencies, *nine states)*[58]

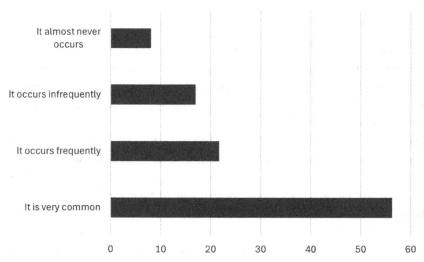

Figure 9 How common is people pretending to be someone else when going to vote? 2008–16
(**Source**: SPAE, 2008–2016 pooled; weighted frequencies, *nine states*)[59]

---

[58] Responses of "Not sure" are removed from this analysis.
[59] Responses of "Not sure" are removed from this analysis.

entire time frame of interest. In 2008, we use the following two questions to measure fraud:

Q37: Vote Theft
Another form of fraud occurs when votes are stolen or tampered with. How frequently do you think this occurs in your community?

Q38: Voter Impersonation
It is illegal for a person to claim to be another person, who is registered to vote, and to cast that person's vote. How often do you think this occurs in your community?

There are five possible responses to all three questions: It is very common; it occurs occasionally; it occurs infrequently; it almost never occurs; or not sure.[60]

There were changes in the question series in 2012, which continued in 2016. The SPAE added fraud questions and placed the new questions in a grid format, instead of separately (Stewart et al., 2016). The question responses remained the same (it is very common to I'm not sure). Two of the questions match closely enough with 2008, so that we can compare perception of fraud over the entire time period.

"The following is a list of activities that are usually against the law. Please indicate how often you think these activities occur *in your county or city.*"

Q29B   People stealing or tampering with ballots that have been voted
Q29C   People pretending to be someone else when going to vote.

Finally, the question also asks about fraud not just in one's county or city. Yet previous work does show that respondents are likely thinking about fraud more broadly than something they saw in their city, county, or community (Atkeson, 2011).

Causal Mechanisms: Why We Expect Election Spending to Affect the Voters and Voting Processes

Political scientist Bridget King (2017, p. 672) writes: "Although citizens physically cast ballots locally, successful elections are a delicate balance between the rules created by state legislatures and their subsequent interpretation and implementation by local election officials." This idea compels King to analyze how

---

[60] The reader who is familiar with the SPAE will notice that there are three fraud questions in 2008. We chose not to use the first question (Question #36) which asks about two types of fraud in the same question (voting more than once and voting when one is not a US citizen). This is a double-barreled question where the researcher cannot ascertain whether the respondent is reporting about one or both of the attitudes. The question also confuses the respondent: What do they say if they perceive one behavior but not the other? In 2012 and 2016, the SPAE inquires about these two concepts in two separate questions.

both voter experience and state-level policies affect voter confidence. As we note in previous sections, local level expenditures are the vast majority of resources used to implement elections. We do not focus on state-level policies in this analysis.[61] Every action taken by local election officials requires some sort of resource. In considering how the county expenditure levels might affect voter confidence or perceptions of fraud, we consider two categories. First, voter experience or those things that the voters may evaluate on election day, which we measure with the SPAE data. Second, there are election ecosystem variables (Huefner et al., 2007; Suttmann-Lea and Merivaki, 2023). Some of these ecosystem factors may be visible to voters and nonvoters, but citizens may never notice them. Some election ecosystem variables are difficult to measure or unavailable in nationwide data such as ours. It is the second category that is the basis for our reasoning that expenditures do not have a linear effect on confidence or belief in fraud.

Voter Experience

Entering a polling place provides the most direct voter experiences that inform public opinion about confidence in the electoral process. In fact, scholars have found extensive evidence that voter experience affects voter confidence. First, political scientists Thad Hall, Quin Monson, and Kelly Patterson (2009), examining the 2008 SPAE, find that the respondent's rating of poll worker performance is positively related to voter confidence (see also Atkeson, 2011). Second, examining the 2012 SPAE, King (2017) finds that respondents who rate the operation of their polling place lower are likely to have lower voter confidence. Third, examining the SPAE from 2008 to 2016, King (2020) finds that reported length of the lines, problems with registration, and problems with voting equipment predict less voter confidence (see also Hale et al., 2015). Theoretically, all five should be related to election spending and are used in our analysis. For example, in the case of pollworkers, scholars and others have long suggested that more training will help improve ratings of pollworkers – which would cost the local election administrator more money. More training would also help the polling place run more smoothly, as would hiring more individuals to answer questions and guide voters on election day. Well-operating voting equipment

---

[61] State policies are not our central concern in this section, but since the effect of county implementation may be affected by the state within which it is located, we choose a statistical model that allows us to take that fact into account. The effect on individual confidence within counties may also vary according to the county in which the individual survey respondent resides because election administrators may use discretion in how they implement those state-level policies. Because of the multiple levels of nesting that are in our data, we use a multilevel or hierarchical statistical model that allows us to take into account both state and county variation in error.

might reduce lines – more maintenance can cost more resources. Making sure that the pollbooks are working well may be out of control of the election administrator, unless they have not hired enough temporary staff to get the final rush of voter registrations entered (for those that do not have online registration), but certainly easily using the pollbooks may necessitate more training – which, again, means more resources. The case of Prince William County Virginia illustrates this point. The county election registrar made errors while preparing the voting machines, resulting in tabulation errors afterward.[62] These errors likely stemmed from a lack of funding creating an environment ripe for human errors (Muzyk, 2024).

These five questions from the SPAE represent the voter experience concepts. Since the SPAE asked these questions from 2008 to 2016, we can see if these concepts are related to expenditures – we hypothesize that the more money spent, the better the voting experience.

How well were things run at the polling place where you voted?

Very well – I did not see any problems at the polling place.

Okay – I saw some minor problems, but nothing that interfered with people voting.

Not well – I saw some minor problems that affected the ability of a few people to vote.

Terrible – I saw some major problems that affected the ability of many people to vote.

I don't know.

Was there a problem with your voter registration when you tried to vote?

Yes (please specify what problem, or problems, you had _____).

No.

I don't know.

Please rate the job performance of the poll workers at the polling place where you voted.

Excellent

Good

Fair

Poor

I don't know

---

[62] The results tapes were not programed to a format that was compatible with state reporting requirements. Attempts to correct this issue appear to have created errors. The reporting errors did not consistently favor one party or candidate but were likely due to a lack of proper planning, a difficult election environment, and human error (Prince William, Office of Elections, 2024).

Approximately, how long did you have to wait in line to vote?

Not at all
Less than 10 minutes
10–30 minutes
31 minutes to 1 hour
More than 1 hour (please specify how long _____)
I don't know

Did you encounter any problems with the voting equipment or the ballot that may have interfered with your ability to cast your vote as intended?

Yes
No
I don't know

Election Ecosystem

The creation of the election ecosystem requires a number of factors, all of which cost resources. These activities include precinct/voting location quality and accessibility, voter education, and whether election officials follow administrative rules. Many ecosystem variables are difficult to measure on a national level and are not included in our statistical analysis. Theoretically, they are important to understanding the totality of expenditures involved in election administration.

What is ironic about the election ecosystem is that some of these factors may promote confidence, while others, if citizens disagree with certain actions, or see them as a waste of money, may actually reduce confidence. Alternatively, we suspect that at the lowest levels of spending, election officials are barely making do – fixing basic problems but not projecting the best run elections. At the lowest levels, as they spend more, we suspect that they will not immediately see increases in confidence or decreases in perceptions of fraud. However, at the lowest levels of spending, even as spending increases, citizens may not notice changes, or they may discount the changes they do notice.

Voter education is one such expenditure which research shows changes the election ecosystem (Suttmann-Lea and Merivaki, 2023). Political scientists Mara Suttmann-Lea and Thessalia Merivaki (2023) show that access to election information increases confidence. They examine the voter information media environment in states and show that more voter information, particularly through social media, increases voter confidence. Jurisdictions around the country may provide different levels of service and this includes voter education.[63] Therefore, we think that variations in spending on voter education may affect confidence among both voters and nonvoters.

Political science professor Matt Barreto and colleagues (2009) conducted a survey of polling places in Los Angeles and found significant variation in the accessibility and quality of polling places. Their teams evaluated polling places on a variety of metrics: "(1) Are polling places easy to find?, (2) Are polling places easy to use and comfortable?, and (3) Are there any barriers to voting in polling places?" (page 448). Barreto and colleagues find that polling place quality affects turnout; we therefore expect the quality of the polling place also affects confidence. This attitude could be quite separate from the measures of voter experience in the SPAE.

In our research in North Carolina, we find that higher-quality election administrators may cost more (Kropf et al., 2020). These "high-quality" election administrators may do things like follow administrative rules (King, 2017) that the citizen either does not see or that they may even evaluate negatively if they do not agree with the purpose.[64] For example, to ensure accuracy, voting locations track voters for postelection audits through a variety of methods such as the authorization to vote slip. Voters are unaware that the election administrators are following procedures and may be displeased at the steps they require them to follow. These steps, and the cost incurred to fulfill them, may not improve the voter's current experience, but does improve other election outcomes.

We also think it is possible that an increase in spending at the lowest levels of spending at first just fixes some basic problems, but as more money is spent or as spending continues at a higher rate, voters gain confidence that the elections are well-run. Alternatively, if voters do not understand the process that election officials must go through, then a low level of spending (perhaps less voter education) may engender a lower level of confidence as spending starts to rise. However, as the different jurisdictions spend more, even those citizens who do not agree with everything a local election official does may nevertheless be confident because the overall ecosystem is good – the polling places are well-marked and easy to find, there are adequate voter education materials, and the overall communication environment may improve confidence.

---

[63] Our conversations with election officials at the 7th Annual Election Science, Reform, and Administration at the University of Georgia confirms this idea. Some election administrators had websites, some did not because of resources and capacity to "create" a website and get info out to voters. One of the Election Administrators mentioned needing help to build a website.

[64] See, for example, Clark, Doug Bock. 2022. "A County Elections Director Stood Up to Locals Who Believe the Voting System is Rigged. They Pushed Back Harder." *Propublica*, October 31. www.propublica.org/article/north-carolina-election-denial-voting-surry, Last accessed April 30, 2023.

Data Analysis

In this section, we examine voter confidence and perception of fraud within the states for which we had the most complete expenditure data (more than 75 percent across the years of analysis).[65] As we noted in Section 1, for expenditures, the year of the national election's expenditure is added to the year prior to create our independent variable – the Election Year-Adjusted Fiscal Years (E-FY).[66] We do so to account for the differences in the timing of financial reporting relative to the national elections that we analyze here.

We combine these data with the SPAE for 2008, 2012, and 2016. The SPAE goes into the field immediately after each presidential election. The SPAE analyzes voter experience as well as a variety of attitudinal and demographic variables such as race, age (continuous in years), education (does the voter have a college degree?), income (categories 1–12), gender (female = 1), and partisanship (1–7, where 7 = strong Republican). We are also able to code for a "winner's effect," which is coded "1" if the respondent was a Democrat in 2008 or 2012 and if the respondent was a Republican in 2016 and zero otherwise.

We analyze the data for each year as one regression model with a variable signifying the year the survey was conducted so we can account for differences that took place each year (year fixed effects; coded either 2008, 2012, or 2016).[67] We decided to run the simplest model in terms of interpretation possible, a linear model[68] with an additional quadratic term (expenditure squared; the squared

---

[65] Alaska runs elections at the state level, and does not report individual borough spending. Thus, we examine the spending for the state as a whole. North Dakota does not run local elections in odd years, and only reports expenditures every two years. To address this, we multiply North Dakota county spending from the election year by 1.833, which is the average proportion of election year to nonelection year spending to account for the two years of spending from the election jurisdictions in the other states. Furthermore, since North Dakota does not have voter registration, we obtained "registered voters" data from North Dakota's "eligible voters" calculation (see https://results.sos.nd .gov/Default.aspx?map=Cty&mode=0, last accessed September 17, 2023). New York City does not report expenditures individually for the boroughs. Thus, we use the City total divided by the City's registered voters for the five boroughs of the City.

[66] Recall from Section 1 that states and localities have differing fiscal year beginning dates.

[67] While there are SPAE data from 2014, we do not include it due the difficulty of calculating the winner's effect. Only one study that we know of analyzes the winner's effect at a lower level than president (Atkeson, 2014). We also do not examine 2020 data mostly because of the Trump effect, but also because of the philanthropic dollars that came to counties all over the country (Brown and Hale, 2023). The philanthropic money would be reported as "expenditures" but would not have come from the county itself.

[68] Many political scientists use linear models for dependent variables with two categories for ease of interpretation (see, for example, Gomila, 2021). But it is not clear that one can use a linear model for four-category variables such as confidence. The perceptive reader will remember that "confidence" is highly skewed with respondents giving positive reports. Over many different types of analysis of the SPAE, we have noticed that "real" changes take place between "Very confident" and "Somewhat confident." Therefore, for a check of the results, we recode the

term models the expectation that expenditure decreases confidence before it increases it).[69] Our dependent variables are the ones reported by individuals: (1) confidence one's ballot is counted and (2) perceptions of fraud. We are most interested in how expenditures affect the individual's responses, so we include expenditure and expenditure-squared, but also control for county size, the individuals' race, age, gender, income, education, partisanship, and whether their party won the contest. Statistically, we need to factor into our analysis that there are individuals in our study who live in the same county, and therefore are similar in many ways, including how the person running elections in their county interprets state laws and rules. Individuals in one county practically have different elections from those in another county – even within the same state. The same may also be true of two respondents to the survey in two different states. Laws and administrative rules vary among states. Scholars conducting statistical analyses have long factored in the idea that different people in different states are clustered (see, for example, Kimball and Kropf, 2005). However, even though scholars know a lot about discretion on the part of local election officials, election scholars have not often factored in the idea that elections are also different among the election jurisdictions within a state.[70]

Analysis

Expenditure's Relationship to Voter Confidence and Perceptions of Fraud

Figures 10 and 11 show the substantive effect (marginal effects) of spending and the nature of that relationship. At the left end of the distribution of spending (lower spending), we observe that as jurisdictions spend more, confidence decreases and perceptions of fraud increase. According to this analysis, jurisdictions that spend approximately $38 per registered voter over two years (about $17/year per registered voter), spending more starts to increase confidence. Similarly, at approximately $38 per registered voter over two years, perceptions of fraud start to decrease.

---

variable into one whose values are "Very confident" or "All the rest." When we code "confidence" empirically into two categories (Very confident versus Other), our results remain the same.

[69] In other analyses of spending's effect on election outcomes, we have discovered that spending's relationship is often not linear, prompting us to hypothesize here that spending might have diminishing marginal returns (related to a steady rise in confidence) or parabolic – that is, perhaps more spending at first has a negative effect on confidence and then at a certain point, a positive effect.

[70] In other words, we run a hierarchical (or multilevel) model because it can account for the correlated error structure at multiple levels. This is not a bug, but a feature of the inherently nested data. As Gelman and Hill (2007, p. 8) note: "the multilevel model provides a coherent model that simultaneously incorporates both individual- and group-level models."

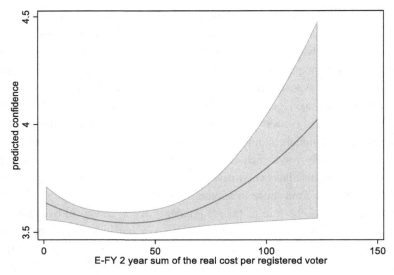

Figure 10 How expenditures affect confidence one's vote counts (2008–16, data weighted)

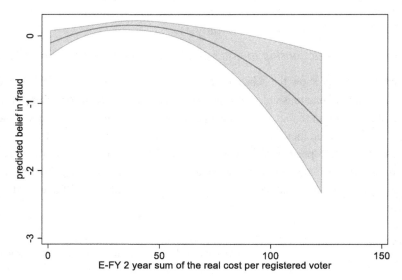

Figure 11 How expenditures affect perceptions of fraud (2008–16, data weighted)

Table 5 contains the regression coefficients used to create Figures 10 and 11; for confidence, we consider only voters, as the question asks whether their vote counts as cast. The analyses show that expenditures affect confidence and

Table 5 Analysis of confidence your ballot counted and perception of fraud

Variables	Confidence ballot counted (higher = more confidence)	Fraud index (higher = more fraud)
Who is examined?	*All voters*	*Voters and nonvoters*
Expenditures (standardized by registered voters; over two years)	−0.005** (0.003)	0.015** (0.006)
Expenditures-squared	0.00007** (0.00003)	−0.0002*** (0.00007)
Voted by mail	−0.154**** (0.027)	*NA (analysis includes voters and nonvoters)*
Income	0.007 (0.005)	−0.016**** (0.004)
Age	.005**** (0.001)	−0.005*** (0.001)
Female	−0.057*** (0.018)	0.021 (0.023)
Race		
Black	0.016 (0.085)	0.223**** (0.058)
Latinx	−0.013 (0.132)	0.046 (0.092)
Asian	0.073* (0.042)	−0.169*** (0.050)
Native American	−0.128* (0.070)	0.260** (0.112)
Mixed	−0.055 (0.070)	−0.199*** (0.074)
Other	0.110 (0.082)	0.137 (0.155)
Middle Eastern	0.363*** (0.119)	−0.286 (0.274)
College degree	0.077**** (0.011)	−0.140*** (0.046)
Winner's effect (presidency)	0.189****	−0.087***

Table 5 (cont.)

Variables	Confidence ballot counted (higher = more confidence)	Fraud index (higher = more fraud)
Who is examined?	*All voters*	*Voters and nonvoters*
	(0.024)	(0.031)
Partisanship (1 very Democrat– 7 very Republican)	−0.028*	0.085
	(0.015)	(0.020)
Natural log of number of registered voters[71]	−0.028***	0.076****
	(0.008)	(0.014)
2012	−0.109*	0.247****
	(0.055)	(0.051)
2016	0.010	0.110***
	(0.033)	(0.032)
Sample size	4,010	3,346
ICC (state)	0.004 (0.006)[72]	0.003 (0.007)[73]
ICC (county)	0.032 (0.016)	0.063 (0.023)
Model fit	−4198.54	−4000.81

$*p < 0.10$; $**p < 0.05$; $***p < 0.01$; $****p < 0.001$; analysis includes weights (inverse probability of ultimate selection).[74] Coefficients are rounded to nearest one-thousandth. Standard errors in parentheses.

perceptions of fraud. We include the tables to show that the findings are consistent with past analyses. For example, the winner's effect is significantly related to both confidence and belief in fraud, controlling for partisanship

---

[71] We also have a variable measuring "rurality" that ranges from 1 to 9 from the Department of Agriculture. We only have the data for 2013, but assuming that degree of rurality does not change much, we substituted "rurality" for the number of registered voters and got substantially similar results.

[72] Since the ICC values are low, we ran an OLS regression and obtained substantially the same results for our main independent variables.

[73] Again, the ICC values are low, so we ran an OLS regression and obtained substantially the same results for our main independent variables.

[74] Scholars question whether the data needs to be weighted in a regression model. The reader will note that weights are created in the SPAE to make the sample be similar on a variety of demographic variables to the target population. That is, the sample may consist of different distributions of the independent variable. Winslip and Radbill (1994) report that "samples with different distributions of the X variables will yield (on average) the same OLS estimates. There is therefore no need for the sample distribution of the X variables to reflect the population distribution" (page 235). And we find that the regressions yield largely similar results. In an abundance of caution, we apply the weights anyway herein.

(a survey measures partisanship asking the respondent to place themselves on a seven-point scale where "1" means they strongly identify with the Democratic Party, and "7," they strongly identify with the Republican Party; winners are coded "1" in 2008 and 2012 if they are Democrats; winners are also Republicans in 2016. All others are "losers," including those who do not lean toward either party). Even controlling for the winner's effect, those who identify as Republican are less likely to be confident, and more likely to believe in fraud. For both, Table 5 shows that those with a college degree and those that are older are more confident, and less likely to perceive there is more fraud. In larger jurisdictions, respondents report a higher perception of fraud and lower level of confidence than in smaller jurisdictions.

For confidence, we find that voters who vote by mail report less confidence, which is consistent with past analyses (see, for example, Bryant, 2020). We decided to run the analyses in Washington only, to see whether expenditures had an effect on confidence in a state where the vast majority of people are voting by mail. We find in the state of Washington that expenditures (and the quadratic term) are not statistically significant. Combined with the fact that those who vote by mail in Table 5 are significantly less confident, the evidence suggests that even more expenditures do not affect confidence in a state where there is universal vote by mail.[75]

Expenditures and Observable Election Outcomes

Regarding the five voter experience variables from the SPAE, we found a linear relationship with one and a nonlinear relationship with another. Expenditures do not affect the other variables. Table 6 shows how spending affects how well the polling place was run, whether there were problems with registration, pollworker ratings, how long the lines were, and whether there were problems with voting equipment.[76] The table shows three of the five "experience" variables are not related to the amount spent on election administration per registered voter in the jurisdiction. Spending is related to line length, but substantively, it is not a strong relationship; spending is related to a reduction in problems with registration, but it is also not a substantively strong relationship. Fewer than 100 voters in this analysis reported problems with registration.

---

[75] These are preliminary results. We invite other scholars to explore this relationship.

[76] We analyze similar regression models as we do for the analysis of confidence and belief in fraud. However, due to potential multicollinearity between the squared and the component term, we first run the quadratic model and report it if there is a significant effect for both the squared and the component term. If one of these terms is not significant, we drop the squared term and report the results of the linear model.

Table 6 Relationship of voter experience variables to amount spent

Variable	Type of relationship	Coefficients
How well was the polling place run?	None	NA
Problems with registration	The more spent, the more problems until about $50/registered voter, then fewer problems	0.002*** (expenditure) (0.0007) −0.00002*** (expenditure squared) (0.000008)
Pollworker ratings	None	NA
Wait time	Linear – the more spent, the shorter the line	−0.005* (expenditure) (0.003)
Voting equipment problems	None	NA

$*p < 0.10$; $p < 0.05$; $**p < 0.01$; $***p < 0.001$; analysis includes weights.
Standard errors in parentheses.

The voter experience variables might have given us a theoretical reason to understand why spending might affect confidence, but since three out of the five are not related to spending, perhaps spending has a more indirect relationship to confidence, or the variables we are unable to observe here are costly for local election officials, creating a potential effect of the spending variables on confidence and belief in fraud. Put another way, the ecosystem created by higher expenditures helps create confidence.

Conclusion

For this first multistate analysis of the effects of expenditures on election administration outcomes, our data show a significant but nonlinear relationship between financial resources and voter perceptions. The models provide evidence that spending affects voter perceptions of the elections. When we graph the results, we see that at first more spending reduces confidence and then more spending is associated with increased confidence to produce a parabolic relationship between spending and confidence. Where perceptions of fraud are concerned, at first, citizens perceive more fraud. As jurisdictions spend more per registered voter, there is a decline in perceptions of fraud. Expenditures are also directly related to how long the lines the voters are reporting with lower wait times reported among jurisdictions that spend more on election administration. Spending also reduces the already very small number of individuals who reported in the SPAE that they had voter registration problems, but this relationship was also nonlinear.

Creating an election ecosystem that induces more confidence may come from election officials' ability to spend more money. More spending may allow for better quality polling places and more educational materials. We wonder if, at the lowest levels of spending, election officials are barely making do. Political science professor Charles Stewart III put it well in a 2022 report in which we (the authors) participated in preparing "The Cost of Conducting Elections."

> Election officials are used to "making do" with what they have. They often express pride in pulling off the complicated logistical maneuvers necessary to conduct elections on a shoestring budget. One consequence of the frugality imposed on election administration is that services provided to voters vary considerably across the nation. (page 1)

But election officials in various jurisdictions judge trade-offs within tight budgets differently (Kropf et al., 2020).[77] For example, we know that some local election officials distribute voter guides and/or make several community presentations to educate voters. Some cannot. We also know that local election officials use social media to educate; some cannot or do not use social media (see, for example, Merivaki and Suttmann-Lea, 2023). We think the result of "barely making do" is that when election administrators begin to spend more, confidence may actually decline before spending increases and confidence increases.

The biggest weakness of our analysis reported here is that comparing spending across counties, townships, and states is a process beset with measurement conflicts. We simply do not know how each jurisdiction reporting spending defines the spending. We know that it is more than just purely the cost of an election, but we have no idea whether various county offices share services such as Human Resources, computing/IT services, or communications. Smaller jurisdictions that make up the majority of election offices may be especially disadvantaged by the lack of resources both within their unit and from being able to get support from other units in their organization. We invite future research using our data or other data collected to see how these relationships play out.

We have not solved the mystery of how much local election jurisdictions should spend on elections, but we do show that spending per registered voter

---

[77] Keep in mind that we are talking here about tough trade-offs that local election officials must make within their election budgets, and not the trade-offs that county legislators must make while budgeting within a county to provide all types of county services such as safety and public health (see McGowan et al., 2021).

results in desirable outcomes such as more confidence and less perception of fraud. Some problems that we encountered are that we are unable to show that spending makes much of a difference in jurisdictions that use mail voting almost exclusively. We expect more research to result from our initial foray into analyzing expenditures.

Conclusion

The title of this Element is *A Republic if You Can Afford It*. How can we not afford the necessary investments in elections administration? A legitimate democracy is not free, nor can we take it for granted. To hold legitimate elections, we have to have personnel and infrastructure, which all cost money. Without this election administration infrastructure, American democracy does not function. At times it seems as if the mechanics of democracy are on a razor's edge, held up only by willing election officials who go above and beyond. However, we have shown that this is not the case everywhere. There are many states that go significantly beyond the minimum in conducting elections and their citizens likely have much more confidence in the election as a result.

Researchers who have examined these issues in the past have been frustrated by the paucity of data on the cost of election administration at the local level, a problem which we have sought to address. In this short Element, we connected election administration with government financial reports and painstakingly worked to collect and check the data. Particularly, we focused on the cost of election administration at the local level and the different ways to measure the cost of election administration. We recommend focusing on "expenditures" because of the balance between data availability and usefulness. We address important issues of election timing versus the timing of the end of fiscal year reporting and introduce the E-FY concept. We described the variation in cost in most of the United States at the local level and how much it varies between states and within states.

Empirically, we show how the cost changes over time and the convergence in spending in the different regions of the country. From a policy perspective, several factors may drive the convergence, such as the use of lower-cost methods of voting, particularly in Western states. However, after the COVID-19 pandemic, many states are now using mail voting and other lower-cost alternatives but almost all election jurisdictions have experienced higher costs for things such as security. We look forward to the analyses of how costs changed during and after the pandemic. We also investigated some of the factors that influence the cost of election administration. Unlike the previous perception of continuous economies of scale, we found with many larger jurisdictions, there is an increasing cost that may be driven by differences in the scope of work performed. These additional costs for large jurisdictions and their states should be examined in more detail in future research.

Finally, we evaluated the connection between financial resources and election administration outcomes such as public perceptions of procedural legitimacy. These findings are critically important as they show that higher spending is associated with greater voter confidence and lower perceptions about fraud. Given the ongoing discussion of decreasing confidence in elections, we think that these results are instructive. We know there is ongoing research about a variety of interventions to increase confidence in elections, but the public should be prepared – many interventions, including voter education, will not be cheap.

Limitations

One of the key limitations, discussed at length herein, is that scholars and policymakers should see our measure of cost as a lower bound on the cost of election administration. While we have done our best to collect election administration expenditures from throughout the United States, we can see that election administration expenditures are different in jurisdictions between states and sometimes even within the same state. Whether it is because expenditures often do not include the full cost of capital or pension expenses, we argue that the expenditure data are simply a lower-bound estimate. County clerks may not divide and charge all of their time in election administration to election administration. In very small jurisdictions where the clerk may be the only full-time personnel and the cost of the clerk's salary may not be included in the election administration expenditure, it becomes even more likely we underestimate election costs. Despite these caveats, we think that the collection and analysis of election administration expenditures throughout the country tells us something important about the influences on election administration spending and the results that come from varying financial resources.

The second major limitation is that the data collection itself varies and it does not vary randomly for most of the states. We were able to collect a significant amount of election administration expenditure data in nine states, but that means that there are forty-one for which we did not have representative data over the time frame. Using data for the states that are not significantly collected can result in sample selection bias. There were four additional states that were complete enough and that did not fail the nonresponse analysis during part of the study period. These states, two of which are in the South, are ideal candidates for future analysis with the collection of additional data. Along with more data collection, the use of imputation – advanced statistical methods that allow one to infer missing values – and other advanced statistical methods may allow scholars to include more states in the analysis between spending and election outcomes.

Another concern might be the lack of control variables, particularly in Section 3. As we were beginning a discussion about expenditures, we specifically chose not to include election results or local election partisanship in our analysis (partisanship variables in Section 4, well-established as affecting public perception of policy). We imagine that there will be great interest in making these comparisons. We caution against this type of analysis without a full suite of controls and complete, representative data. We recommend focusing on a limited number of states like we have done here that are representative of states throughout the United States.

Along with the specification of any models to include additional controls, we expect to see more refined statistical modeling. We have mostly used multilevel or hierarchical models because of the multiple nesting of data but scholars can pursue some of the many other statistical modeling strategies available. One of the major limitations of some of our data analysis is that we are simply establishing associations. We look forward to seeing more advanced causal modeling strategies. Also, there may also be a spatial pattern in the data, and changes in spending by local election jurisdictions may occur as people move throughout the United States changing the underlying property tax base, which all suggest that spatial analysis of election cost data would be another valuable type of analysis.

Extending the Research Agenda

The analysis of data between 2008 and 2016 was fortunate as those were reasonably routine times for election administration, which means that the connection between resources and outcomes was likely only influenced by fewer resources due to the exogenous stress of the Great Recession. In many ways, the recession is an interesting "shock" that significantly reduced resources throughout the country. In contrast, the election administration response to the COVID-19 pandemic exogenously influenced election processes, which may be exploited to determine a causal effect of changing election processes on cost. Therefore, one of the most important needs for research and policy is to collect election cost data from 2017 to the present. These data can show how COVID-19 and the 2020 election changed the election administration cost function. It will be interesting to see if the convergence across regions that we noted in Section 2 continues after 2020.

Future scholars and policymakers should analyze other policy and administrative changes. Factors such as shifting to mail balloting or vote centers may reduce the cost of elections significantly, but it may require additional planning

and administration throughout the year. Some jurisdictions may require significantly more office space in which to sort through and verify mailed ballots.
Switching to all-paper ballots is likely to significantly increase both the cost of
particular elections and the broader cost of election administration. We think
that scholars should analyze administrative changes as both a cause and conse-
quence of changes in election administration resources. Changes in laws in
some states, such as the inclusion of voter ID, may also influence election
administration costs.

In terms of election outcomes that scholars could connect with the election
funding cost data, there are many outcomes to consider. While we looked at
perceptual measures of the functioning of the election, scholars could analyze
residual votes and voter turnout more, as well as line length and a variety of
other outcomes. One area that may be particularly interesting to the accounting
and management community is exploring the connection between resources
spent on election administration and election audit findings.

Scholars should also consider some items related to election expenditure
when developing a broad election resources research agenda. We are particularly interested in human resources – administrators and pollworkers. We have
begun the study of election administration salaries and benefits. These human
resource costs are often some of the biggest costs of government. Yet recruit-
ment of workers is costly and time-intensive, and especially concerning in an
era when some individuals are attacking election officials – verbally and
physically. We encourage further exploration of succession planning and career-
development strategies to increase the election workforce.

Finally, we need further cost analysis within election jurisdictions. What is
driving administrative costs? Is it human resource costs or is it technology?
What are the costs of different forms of voting? These are difficult to answer
when we are only able to examine total cost in many places, and many places
have multiple types of voting. Ideally, we would use cost accounting methods to
determine both the direct and the indirect costs of different types of voting as
has been done in countries outside of the United States (Krimmer et al., 2021).
At this point, the AFRs provide some of this information, but often the type of
election administration cost data we care most about may not be readily
available.

Implications for Policy and Practice

Charles Stewart pointed out that the difference in expenditure between the
lowest spending jurisdictions is nearly an order of magnitude different from
the highest spending jurisdictions. We think that we have explained why this

may be and show that there is likely to be an impact on voter perceptions of the outcome of elections. What we have avoided is prescriptions for policy. We do not know if the lowest-spending jurisdictions actually are spending too little, or the highest-spending, too much. In fact, given the nonlinear relationship between spending and the confidence and perceptions of fraud outcomes, the election administrators in some low-spending jurisdictions may be loath to increase spending if it is perceived that they are wasting resources. This research cannot tell us how much we should spend on election administration. What it can show us, though, are the trends and provide a basis for elections policy and practice discussions to proceed.

One of the most interesting things that jumps out of the data is the trends in the election costs that we discussed in Section 2, particularly the differences by region. It is amazing how much spending on elections administration has declined in the West. This may be because of election administration changes in voting that need fewer resources, or it could be because of fiscal stress in these states. Election administrators and local budget and finance staff will likely want to discuss these trends. This trend stands in stark contrast to the South where election administration expenditures have increased significantly over time. Assuming that the election changes in the West are what are driving the expenditure declines, election policy and practice may want to study some of the changes that have been implemented in the West.

It is likely to be disappointing to some that we are unwilling to say how much should be spent on election administration. We believe that we need more analysis of spending by different groups and by the different levels of government. Our research fills a needed gap in the cost of elections administration at the local level. Given that we know increasingly more about the disparity and inconsistent nature of election funding, the normative question of should higher levels of government subsidize election administration is an important policy question. Certainly, public finance theory tells us that the federal government does have a role to play in stabilization and, given the critical nature of election administration, one could make a strong case on a theoretical basis that the federal government may need to stabilize election spending during times of exogenous shocks such as recessions or pandemics. This is especially true given that most states now are banning the private financing of election administration.

Overall, we think that the trends and relationships that we have uncovered justify further research investments in this area so that policy can be informed by data and not opinions driven by political agendas. Attacks by foreign actors on election administration infrastructure suggest that there is a need for a larger national investment and external forces such as recessions and pandemics may also necessitate a federal response. At the same time, we may not want national political actors to be able to direct local election administration. These are difficult normative issues but sensible policy proposals such as those put forward by Charles Stewart (2022) and others may provide reasonable ways forward. Election administration takes significant financial resources, but these resource needs are not insurmountable. Funding election administration will continue to challenge policymakers at all levels of government, and we hope this work contributes to that conversation.

References

Adcock, R., & Collier, D. (2001). Measurement validity: A shared standard for qualitative and quantitative research. *American Political Science Review, 95*(3), 529–546.

Aiyede, E. R., & Aregbeyen, O. (2012). The cost of the 2011 general elections in Nigeria. *Journal of African Elections, 11*(1), 136–152.

Ansolabehere, S., & Persily, N. (2007). Vote fraud in the eye of the beholder: The role of public opinion in the challenge to voter identification requirements. *Harvard Law Review, 121*, 1737–1774.

Atkeson, L. R. (2011). Voter confidence in 2010: Voter identification, perceptions of fraud, winning and losing and the voting experience (Caltech/MIT Voting Technology Project, VTP Working Paper #103). https://dspace.mit.edu/bitstream/handle/1721.1/97654/WP_103.pdf;sequence=1.

Atkeson, L. R. (2014). Voter confidence in 2010: Local, state, and national factors. In R. M. Alvarez & B. Grofman (Eds.), *Election administration in the United States: The state of reform ten years after Bush v. Gore* (pp. 253–278). Cambridge University Press.

Atkeson, L. R., Alvarez, R. M., & Hall, T. E. (2015). Voter confidence: How to measure it and how it differs from government support. *Election Law Journal, 14*(3), 207–219.

Barreto, M. A., Cohen-Marks, M., & Woods, N. D. (2009). Are all precincts created equal? The prevalence of low-quality precincts in low-income and minority communities. *Political Research Quarterly, 62*(3), 445–458.

Brace, K. (2013). "Basic election administration facts PowerPoint." www.electiondataservices.com/research-services/, last accessed July 5, 2018.

Brennan Center. (2006). The machinery of democracy: Voting system security, accessibility, usability, and cost. Brennan Center for Justice at NYU Law School. Technical Report.

Brown, M., & Hale, K. (2023). The new role of philanthropy in supporting election administration in the 2020 election. In D. Tran (Ed.), *Pandemic at the polls: How the politics of COVID-19 played into American elections* (pp. 139–157). Lexington Books.

Bryant, L. (2020). Seeing is believing: An experiment on absentee ballots and voter confidence (Part of a special symposium on election sciences). *American Politics Research, 48*(6), 700–704. https://doi.org/10.1177/1532673X20922529.

Burden, B. C., et al. (2012). The effect of administrative burden on bureaucratic perception of policies: Evidence from election administration. *Public Administration Review, 72*(5), 741–751.

Burden, B. C., & Neiheisel, J. R. (2013). Election administration and the pure effect of voter registration on turnout. *Political Research Quarterly, 66*(1), 77–90. https://doi.org/10.1177/1065912911430671.

Burden, B. C., & Stewart, C., III. (2014). Introduction to the measure of American elections. In B. C. Burden & C. Stewart III (Eds.), *The measure of American elections* (pp. 1–39). Cambridge University Press.

Caltech–MIT Voting Technology Project. (2001). Voting – what is, what could be. www.vote.caltech.edu/2001report.htm.

Crawford v. Marion County. (2008). 533US 181. www.oyez.org/cases/2007/07–21.

DeNardo, J. (1980). Turnout and the vote: The joke's on the Democrats. *American Political Science Review, 74*(2), 406–420.

Durning, A. (2023). Idaho, Montana, and Washington could save $30 million by moving local elections to national election day. *Sightline Institute.* www.sightline.org/2023/07/05/idaho-montana-and-washington-could-save-30-million-by-moving-local-elections-to-national-election-day/.

Finkler, S. A., Calabrese, T. D., & Smith, D. L. (2022). *Financial management for public, health, and not-for-profit organizations.* CQ Press.

Folz, D. H. (2014). Vote centers as a strategy to control election administration costs: Findings from a pilot project. *SAGE Open, 4* (1, January–March), 1–10.

Gelman, A., & Hill, J. (2007). *Data analysis using regression and multilevel/hierarchical models* (Vol. 1). Cambridge University Press.

Gomez, B. T., Hansford, T. G., & Krause, G. A. (2007). The Republicans should pray for rain: Weather, turnout, and voting in US presidential elections. *Journal of Politics, 69*(3), 649–663.

Gomila, R. (2021). Logistic or linear? Estimating causal effects of experimental treatments on binary outcomes using regression analysis. *Journal of Experimental Psychology: General, 150*(4), 700–709. https://doi.org/10.1037/xge0000920.

Granof, M. H., & Khumawala, S. (2013). *Government and not for profit accounting* (6th ed.). John Wiley & Sons.

Gronke, P. (2014). Voter confidence as a metric of election performance. In B. C. Burden & C. Stewart III (Eds.), *The measure of American elections* (pp. 248–270). Cambridge University Press.

Hale, K., Montjoy, R., & Brown, M. (2015). *Administered elections: How American elections work.* Palgrave MacMillan.

Hall, T. E., Monson, J. Q., & Patterson, K. D. (2009). The human dimension of elections: How poll workers shape public confidence in elections. *Political Research Quarterly, 62*(3), 507–522. https://doi.org/10.1177/1065912908 324870.

Hamilton, R. H. (1988). American all-mail balloting: A decade's experience. *Public Administration Review, 48*, 860–866.

Hanushek, E. A. (1997). Assessing the effects of school resources on student performance: An update. *Educational Evaluation and Policy Analysis, 19*(2), 141–164.

Hawkins, E. (2001). "Cost and finance of elections." Paper presented to CalTech-MIT Voting Technology Conference 2001, March 30, http://people.hss.caltech .edu/~voting/hawkins_present.pdf, last accessed February 18, 2015.

Hill, S. A. (2012). Election administration finance in California counties. *The American Review of Public Administration, 42*(5), 606–628.

Horngren, C., Datar, T., & Rajan, M. (2012). *Cost accounting: A managerial emphasis*. Prentice-Hall.

Huefner, S. F., Tokaji, D. P., & Cemenska, N. A. (2007). *From registration to recounts: The election ecosystems of five midwestern states*. Moritz College of Law at The Ohio State University. https://law.osu.edu/electionlaw/pro jects/registration-to-recounts/toc.pdf.

James, T. S., & Jervier, T. (2017). The cost of elections: The effects of public sector austerity on electoral integrity and voter engagement. *Public Money & Management, 37*, 461–468.

Keyssar, A. (2009). *The right to vote: The contested history of democracy in the United States*. Basic Books.

Kimball, D. C., & Kropf, M. (2005). Ballot design and unrecorded votes on paper-based ballots. *Public Opinion Quarterly, 69*(4), 508–529.

King, B. A. (2017). Policy and precinct: Citizen evaluations and electoral confidence. *Social Science Quarterly, 98*(2), 672–689. https://doi.org/ 10.1111/ssqu.12303.

King, B. A. (2020). Waiting to vote: The effect of administrative irregularities at polling locations and voter confidence. *Policy Studies, 41*(2–3), 230–248. https://doi.org/10.1080/01442872.2019.1694652.

King, G., Keohane, R. O., & Verba, S. (1994). *Designing social inquiry: Scientific inference in qualitative research*. Princeton University Press.

Kousser, J. M. (1974). *The shaping of southern politics*. Yale University Press.

Krimmer, R., Duenas-Cid, D., & Krivonosova, I. (2021). New methodology for calculating cost-efficiency of different ways of voting: Is internet voting cheaper? *Public Money & Management, 41*(1), 17–26.

Kropf, M. (2005). Dogs and dead people: Incremental election reform in Missouri. In D. J. Palazzollo & J. W. Ceaser (Eds.), *Election reform: Politics and policy* (pp. 157–173). Lexington Books.

Kropf, M. (2016). *Institutions and the right to vote in America*. Palgrave.

Kropf, M. (2024). The pandemic voting experience. In D. Tran (Ed.), *Pandemic at the polls: How the politics of COVID-19 played into American elections* (pp. 19–32). Lexington Books.

Kropf, M., & Pope, J. V. (2020). Election costs: A study of North Carolina. In M. Brown, K. Hale, & B. King (Eds.), *The future of election administration* (pp. 185–198). Palgrave.

Kropf, M., Pope, J. V., Shepherd, M. J., & Mohr, Z. (2020). Making every vote count: The important role of managerial capacity in achieving better election administration outcomes. *Public Administration Review, 80*(5), 733–742.

Lamb, M. (2021). The "costs" of voting: The effects of vote-by-mail on election administration finance in Colorado. *Social Science Quarterly, 102*(4), 1361–1379. https://doi.org/10.1111/ssqu.13012.

López-Pintor, R., & Fischer, J. (2005). *Cost of registration and elections (CORE) project*. Center for Transitional and Post-Conflict Governance.

McCulloch, S. (2022). INFLATE: Stata module to inflate variables to real dollars using the CPI-U series (Statistical Software Components No. S459037). Boston College Department of Economics.

McGowan, M. J., Pope, J. V., Kropf, M., & Mohr, Z. (2021). Guns or butter . . . or elections? Understanding intertemporal and distributive dimensions of policy choice through the examination of budgetary tradeoffs at the local level. *Public Budgeting & Finance, 41*(4), 3–19. https://doi.org/10.1111/pbaf.12296.

Merivaki, T., & Suttmann-Lea, M. (2023). Can electoral management bodies expand the pool of registered voters? Examining the effects of face-to-face, remote, traditional, and social media outreach. *Policy Studies, 44*(3), 377–407. https://doi.org/10.1080/01442872.2022.2044020.

Mohr, Z. (2017). *Cost accounting in government: Theory and applications*. Taylor & Francis.

Mohr, Z., Pope, J. V., Kropf, M., & Shepherd, M. J. (2018). "Does Politics Influence Election Administration Expenditure? A Political Model of Election Administration Expenditure in North Carolina Counties." Paper presented at the 2018 Southern Political Science Association, New Orleans.

Mohr, Z., Pope, J. V., Kropf, M., & Shepherd, M. J. (2019). Strategic spending: Does politics influence election administration expenditure? *American Journal of Political Science, 63*(2), 427–438. https://doi.org/10.1111/ajps.12422.

Mohr, Z., Pope, J. V., Shepherd, M. J., Kropf, M., & Hill, A. (2020). Evaluating the recessionary impact on election administration budgeting and spending. *American Politics Research*, *48*(6), 709–713. https://doi.org/10.1177/1532673x20935785.

Montjoy, Robert S. (2010). The changing nature ... and costs ... of election administration. *Public Administration Review*, *70*, 867–875.

Muzyk, Cher. (2024, Jan 11). Criminal charges against former Prince William elections chief – now dropped – stemmed from vote tabulation errors. *Prince William Times*. https://www.princewilliamtimes.com/news/criminal-charges-against-former-prince-william-elections-chief-now-dropped-stemmed-from-vote-tabulation-errors/article_40a3eeca-b0e9-11ee-b49c-4f4ae054a6b0.html

National Research Council. (2006). Aspects of the role of cost in voting system performance (Chapter 6). In *Aspects of state voter registration databases* (pp. 93–99). The National Academies Press. https://doi.org/10.17226/11666.

NCSL (2018). "The price of democracy: Splitting the bill for elections." *National Conference of State Legislatures*.

NCSL (2023). "Summary: Vote Centers." Published by the National Conference of State Legislatures. www.ncsl.org/elections-and-campaigns/vote-centers.

Norden, L., Cortes, E., & Howard, E. (2020). Estimated Costs of Covid-19 Election Resiliency Measures. *Brennan Center for Justice at New York University School of Law*.

Pressman, J. L., & Wildavsky, A. B. (1984). *Implementation*. University of California Press.

Sances, M. W., & Stewart III, C. (2015). Partisanship and confidence in the vote count: Evidence from US national elections since 2000. *Electoral Studies*, *40*, 176–188. https://doi.org/10.1016/j.electstud.2015.08.004.

Schur, L., Ameri, M., & Adya, M. (2017). Disability, voter turnout, and polling place accessibility. *Social Science Quarterly*, *98*, 1374–1390.

Sinclair, B., Smithy, S. S., & Tucker, P. D. (2019). "It's largely a rigged system": Voter confidence and the winner effect in 2016. *Political Research Quarterly*, *71*(4), 854–868. https://doi.org/10.1177/1065912918768006.

Stein, R., & Vonnahme, G. (2009). *The cost of elections*. Rice University. Unpublished manuscript.

Stein, R. M., & Vonnahme, G. (2012). When, where, and how we vote: Does it Matter? *Social Science Quarterly*, *93*(3), 692–712.

Stewart, C. (2013a). 2008 Survey of the performance of American elections. https://doi.org/10.7910/DVN/1FYT4P, Harvard Dataverse.

Stewart, C. (2013b). 2012 Survey of the performance of American elections. https://doi.org/10.7910/DVN/WP8RHI, Harvard Dataverse.

Stewart, C. (2017). 2016 Survey of the performance of American elections. https://doi.org/10.7910/DVN/Y38VIQ, Harvard Dataverse.

Stewart III, C. (2022). The cost of conducting elections. Technical report. https://electionlab.mit.edu/sites/default/files/2022-05/TheCostofConductingElections-2022.pdf.

Stewart, C., Ansolabehere, S., & Persily, N. (2016). Revisiting public opinion on voter identification and voter fraud in an era of increasing partisan polarization. *Stanford Law Review, 68*(June), 1455–1489.

Suttmann-Lea, M., & Merivaki, T. (2023). The impact of voter education on voter confidence: Evidence from the 2020 US presidential election. *Election Law Journal, 22*(2), 145–165.

Tyler, T. R. (2006). *Why people obey the law*, Princeton University Press.

Winship, C., & Radbill, L. (1994). Sampling weights and regression analysis. *Sociological Methods & Research* 23(2): 230–257. https://doi.org/10.1177/0049124194023002004.

Acknowledgments

No one ever collected local election administration cost data for the entire United States before we decided to try. That should have been fair warning against attempting it, but we did. This project and the Element, that is, its conclusion, were a journey. We started with only a vague idea of our destination – good, national, election cost data – and only some idea of the stops along the way. It ended up being longer, more difficult, and even more dangerous (thank you COVID) than we could have ever imagined. Like any journey, this project would not have been possible without the help and assistance of many people.

First, we acknowledge the work of our fabulous graduate assistants Madison Esterle and Rob Austin, who painstakingly collected the election cost data from the local government AFRs. They had to try to collect the reports from thousands of local governments. They had to search within these documents, which are often hundreds of pages long, to find the cost that pertained to election administration. They had to copy and sometimes add up figures to make sure the cost reported is the cost that we wanted. They had to go back and audit the data. It was a painstaking work, and we truly appreciate you. We will never forget your humor and good natures as you sorted through these mind-numbingly technical documents.

Second, we acknowledge our funders. Charles Stewart and the MIT Election Data and Science Lab (MEDSL) funded the data collection efforts through two New Initiatives grants in 2017 and 2018. Without this funding, we would not have been able to hire people to collect data. We also acknowledge significant support from the University of North Carolina at Charlotte. They provided the facilities for our work. They also provided time for Martha to complete a critical part of merging the election cost data with registered votes and ballots cast. Reese Manceneaux, UNC Charlotte's data services librarian, went above and beyond the call of duty on several occasions helping us with our data.

Third, we thank our spouses and friends who have helped in a variety of ways. Ashley Mohr listened to a lot of things that she does not care about (she cares about the elections but not the accounting). We thank Dr. John Szmer for being an encouraging spouse to Martha and colleague and friend to the other coauthors. We thank Mary Jo's children who at least pretended to be interested in what their mom was researching, but mostly she appreciates that they learned the importance of elections. We also appreciate the many professional colleagues and friends that provided insight and assistance as we presented preliminary findings. Also, we thank two anonymous reviewers for their helpful comments, as well as our colleagues who commented on our draft at the North Carolina Political Science Association, Dr. Christopher Cooper (Western Carolina University), Dr. Mitchell Brown (Auburn University), and Dr. Nadine Gibson (UNC Wilmington).

Last but not least, we acknowledge the scores of local government officials that have assisted us, especially Mecklenburg County, North Carolina's Michael Dickerson, and Kristin Mavromatis. Local government professionals throughout the country have answered our many questions about election administration and local government budgeting and accounting. We would not have had many of the insights, or in some cases known the limits of what is possible, without your help. You make American democracy and government work. This Element would not have happened without you.

Cambridge Elements ☰

Campaigns and Elections

R. Michael Alvarez
California Institute of Technology

R. Michael Alvarez is Professor of Political and Computational Social Science at Caltech. His current research focuses on election administration and technology, campaigns and elections, and computational modeling.

Emily Beaulieu Bacchus
University of Kentucky

Emily Beaulieu Bacchus is Associate Professor of Political Science and Director of International Studies at the University of Kentucky. She is an expert in political institutions and contentious politics—focusing much of her work on perceptions of election fraud and electoral protests. Electoral Protest and Democracy in the Developing World was published with Cambridge University Press in 2014.

Charles Stewart III
Massachusetts Institute of Technology

Charles Stewart III is the Kenan Sahin Distinguished Professor of Political Science at MIT. His research and teaching focus on American politics, election administration, and legislative politics.

About the Series

Broadly focused, covering electoral campaigns and strategies, voting behavior, and electoral institutions, this Elements series offers the opportunity to publish work from new and emerging fields, especially those at the interface of technology, elections, and global electoral trends.

Cambridge Elements ☰

Campaigns and Elections

Elements in the Series

Securing American Elections: How Data-Driven Election Monitoring Can Improve Our Democracy
R. Michael Alvarez, Nicholas Adams-Cohen, Seo-young Silvia Kim and Yimeng Li

The Power of Polls: A Cross-National Experimental Analysis of the Effects of Campaign Polls
Jason Roy, Shane P. Singh and Patrick Fournier

The Representational Consequences of Electronic Voting Reform: Evidence from Argentina
Santiago Alles, Tiffany D. Barnes and Carolina Tchintian

The Social Origins of Electoral Participation in Emerging Democracies
Danielle F. Jung and James D. Long

Elections and Satisfaction with Democracy: Citizens, Processes and Outcomes
Jean-François Daoust and Richard Nadeau

Citizens Under Compulsory Voting: A Three-Country Study
Ruth Dassonneville, Thiago Barbosa, André Blais, Ian McAllister and Mathieu Turgeon

Storefront Campaigning
Joshua P. Darr and Sean Whyard

A Republic If You Can Afford It: How Much Does It Cost to Administer Elections?
Zachary Mohr, Martha E. Kropf, Mary Jo McGowan and JoEllen V. Pope

A full series listing is available at: www.cambridge.org/ECEP

Printed in the United States
by Baker & Taylor Publisher Services